Jules Delorme

faller

BookLand press

Published by
BookLand Press Inc.
15 Allstate Parkway
Suite 600
Markham, Ontario L3R 5B4
www.booklandpress.com

Printed in Canada

Front cover image by Jennifer Deschamps

Library and Archives Canada Cataloguing in Publication

Title: Faller / Jules Delorme.
Names: Delorme, Jules, author.
Description: Series statement: Modern Indigenous voices
Identifiers: Canadiana (print) 20220410690 | Canadiana (ebook)
20220410712 | ISBN 9781772311747 (softcover) |
ISBN 9781772311754 (EPUB)
Subjects: LCGFT: Poetry.
Classification: LCC PS8607.E487565 F35 2022 | DDC C811/.6 — dc23

We acknowledge the support of the Government of Canada through the Canada Book Fund and the support of the Ontario Arts Council, an agency of the Government of Ontario. We also acknowledge the support of the Canada Council for the Arts.

*To the better angels in my life. The many warriors,
most of them women, stronger than me.
I wish I could name you all. There have been so many.
And I am grateful every single day.*

Table of Contents

Ohkwá:ri | 7

Silence | 12

The Boy | 16

Moccasin Face | 27

Dianne | 35

Faller | 45

The River | 52

Killer | 55

Suckers | 63

Goat | 72

The Broken Man | 75

The Man | 82

Truth | 90

Gun | 93

How Crow Made Human Beings | 99

Following | 103

Tending Memory | 105

Bear | 114

Ohkwá:ri

There was this Bear.
This Ohkwá:ri
A long time ago.
Way back.
Before there was too much of everything.
This Bear.
Not a good Bear or a bad Bear.
Just a Bear.
For most of her life this Ohkwá:ri had it alright.
She was the only Bear around.
I don't know if she was the only Bear in the whole world
or anything,
but she was the only one around in those parts.
Nothing messed with her.
She just went around doing her thing.
Being a Bear.
But then one day people started to show up.
Everybody knows how that goes.
Just a few many at first. Then a few more.
And then more and more until there are so many
you can't even keep count.
The way it always goes with people.
At first the people just did their own thing.
Hunted and fished. Planted some corn.
Stayed away from the Bear.
But then, when there was enough of them to do something
they started to talk about the Bear.
She was dangerous they said. She was stealing their food.

They said all kinds of things because they were scared of
her. She never did anything to them but she was
an Ohkwá:ri and they were just people.
Ohkwá:ri don't exactly have to put up with a lot of crap.
The people got together and made their plans and then
they went after the Bear. They went out into the woods
and tried to kill her but she fought and she was a Bear.
The ones that survived ran away.
Now the people had a good reason to be scared of the Bear.
They made more plans. New plans.
They dug a pit and managed to trap her in it.
She put up a hell of a fight.
Dragged some of them down into that hole with her.
But in the end once the Bear fell down
in that hole it was over.
People came from miles around to look at her.
Stare down at her.
She put up a big fuss at first.
Kept trying to get out of that hole and fight.
But after a while she just gave up.
Whatever it was that made her an Ohkwá:ri went away
and all she could do was wait down there in that pit to die.
They threw down food but she wouldn't eat.
They threw rocks at her and she wouldn't move.
After a while the people stopped coming to look at her.
Everything about her that was Ohkwá:ri everything
that used to scare them was gone.
So they just left her in the pit to die.
It took a long time. Even Bears that don't remember
how to be Bears don't die too easy.
She rotted there in that pit for a real long time.

When she finally did die the people barely noticed.
She was so skinny by then they couldn't even get any meat
off her so they just piled dirt to fill in the hole to cover
over the smell and got on with their lives.
They forgot what it was like to have an Ohkwá:ri around.
To be scared.
To be in awe.
To have something be bigger and stronger than them.
The people didn't know it but they lost something when
they dug that hole and trapped the Bear in it.
They never even knew what it was they lost
or why they lost it.
They never knew anything got lost.
Just some dead skinny Bear stinking up
a hole in the ground.
Far as they could see the world was a safer place a lot
easier place without that Ohkwá:ri lurking out
there in the woods.
They slept better at night.
They didn't have any more nightmares.
They didn't jump at every sound.
They felt safe.
That's all that mattered they thought.
It's not like their lives fell to pieces or anything.
The sky and the sun and the stars stayed right up there
where they always were.
The world kept right on moving.
But they lost something. The people.
Something that was supposed to be a part their lives.
Their dreams.
Their nightmares.

When the people trapped that bear they lost that thing
whatever it is that makes stories worth telling.
Maybe stories don't seem too important.
Maybe dreams don't seem important either.
Not as important as being safe or
maybe living a little bit longer.
Not things you can hold in your hands or trade or sell.
Add up in some book.
Figure out on some computer.
But that Ohkwá:ri belonged.
She was supposed to be there.
When she was gone everything was different.
Cleaner maybe.
Brighter. Safer.
But not nearly as…
Not nearly so…
What?
I don't know.
I can't remember that part.
I can't remember it.
The ending.
How it ends.
I can never remember the whole story.
It happened a long time ago.
Just some story that happened a long time ago.
I still remember bits of it though.
I don't know why.
But I remember little bits of that story all the time.
I can't tell it all the way to the end not the way
that I heard it.
But I remember pieces of it.
I forget a whole lot of things but I've still got pieces
of that story stuck inside me.

I don't know why.
I don't remember why.
Just those pieces stuck inside of me.
It means something.
I used to know it all the way to the end but
I can't remember enough of it to put into words anymore.
I used to know all the stories and now I don't know
any of them all the way to the end anymore.
I remember them being told.
The way that people told it.
But chunks of them keep rotting away.
Decomposing.
That Bear though.
Something about that Ohkwá:ri.
I never forget about that bear…

Silence

there is the story.
the telling of the story.
there is the listening.
and there is the silence. when no story is being told.
there is the making of music.
there is the dancing and the singing and the listening.
and there is the silence. The silence that lies beyond the reach
of any music or any voice.
this thing, this third thing is not known to many.
it is forgotten by even more.
and that is what gives it its power.
sometimes it lives in the light.
sometimes it lives in the darkness.
some are born with the darkness of this thing,
this shadowed silence, swimming with them inside the womb.
and when they are born their spines do not straighten up
as easily as others and they find it harder to walk and when
they do walk they fall down again and again. if they find the
strength to stand then this thing, this thing that even they
cannot see or know that it is there, but they suspect is there,
has always been there, they have some hidden thought that
perhaps this is the way that the world must be, that this thing
would knock them down or drag them down and if they
crawl back up then it will do the
same thing again and again.
and again.
and again.
this dark silence.

for some of these people if they open up their mouths to speak then they will find that the words have been strangled. smothered. buried. deep deep down inside of them even before these words could be given birth. and so they, these people, most of them, fall silent, remain silent, for this hint of a feeling inside of them tells them that it is useless and fruitless to even try, because the words will never be able to leave their mouths fully alive or alive in any way that matters. when The Black Robes came they had with them a book that said that the word was the beginning. and yet this book also said that their god was too large, too vast and unknowable for mere words to encompass.
there are some things that are too large for the minds and mouths of mere human beings to grasp. The Black Robes had that much right.
but it is not just their god or anyone else's gods that live beyond the words. it is other things too. it is those things that make us silent. not in awe or in reverence, but because the silence is so much larger than we can understand and because the words and the music have been taken away, strangled stillborn inside of us, and we fall silent because we have no other choice, because we have nothing at all to offer the world that has not already been offered in a better and more truthful and more substantial way.
that emptiness also is too large for words
or understanding or meaning.
we stay silent. we fall down or we do not even ever rise up, not because we feel the power of things moving through us but because we feel nothing at all, because our throats and our legs and our hearts and our stomachs are numb and frozen and horribly unspeakably empty.

i know.
i know.
i can feel it just out of reach, too large for any words. and my
thoughts can form but they will not survive. they desperately
seek some kind of shape, but the shapes that will not hold in
fullness or declination, mere ghosts of the stories that desire
so very much to be told.
i know.
i cannot speak these things.
but i know.
i try to stand and i fall down again and again because my body
and my brain have been beaten down by men.
but also because i was born to fall down.
i was born with part of me already long ago dead and i can
wrestle down these dead words, but they will never be enough.
they will never be the story.
not the whole story.
i know.
those others see only the mangled form, the scarred and
wordless form that is called the body today, a body that
stumbles and stutters and falls down on the ground frothing
at the mouth. but they cannot see the rest.
they cannot see me and they cannot hear me.
they cannot hear the hidden me or see the hidden me because
he was strangled mute and contorted in the womb and so
he lurks so deep down inside of this scarred, stumbling and
stammering shell.
this is not the telling of my story.
this is not the music, the song or the drumming of my song.
this is what is left of me when everything else, all the stories and
all the music have gone silent, have been taken away from me.

this is the dark silence.
this is the voice of a dying animal in its cage.
strangled.
numb.
too small and starved and desiccated to be anything like the
real thing.
this is not the telling of my story.
it is dead words on a dead page, perhaps on dying leaves
of paper, just dying dead bits of shadows, with the stink of
death still upon them.
this is all that there is left to my story.
there may be no one out there to listen.
there may be nothing left inside me to be worth
the hearing of it.
but i will tell what i can.
i will stumble and i will fall and i may never escape the con-
fines of this nothing, these fragments of a trapped and bitter
mind. this black silence, but i will tell it.
i will try to tell it.
i will try again and again and fail and fall again and again,
hurl my body against the walls of this cage that i am trapped
in, until this dead or dying thing has been told.
it may signify nothing at all.
in the end, after all the sound and the fury, it will almost
certainly signify nothing.
but i will tell it.
i will try to tell it.
it is not the telling of my story.
but it will be something.
it will be something like the telling of a story.
and that, even that, will be better than the silence.
anything, anything at all, will be better than the silence.

The Boy

I see him walking across the field, through the patches of dried out tall grass, the rotted out rusted corpses of cars and tractor parts that have been there for as long as I remembered, for what seems like as long as anybody remembered. I'm not sure he's real. I'm not sure he's human. He looks like some kind of monster, like some kind of beast from an old TV movie the old people's stories with the strange shuffling limp and scarred shaved bald head, bare in the hot summer sun, shining in some places and dull in others.
Nobody on the Rez walks around with a bare head in the middle of summer.
Sometimes old Pieface Tim comes wandering over from next door, forgetting where he lives, but he has all his hair except for in one spot on the side of his head where somebody hit him with a rock from a campfire and he always wears a Canadian Tire cap.
This one's definitely not old Pieface.
Even old Pieface looks like a human being at first look.
I don't have any particular feeling about this not stranger or about what he might do.
It's hot and I'm bored and I'm tired.
I'm always tired. The doctors said I would get tired.
I don't think that he's going to ease my boredom or make me not tired in any way that matters, even if he's some kind of real monster.
When I tell the story later on if I live I'll probably say that I felt his presence as I stood there and knew that he was going to have a profound effect upon on my world.

But it won't be true. It'll be a Rez truth. Sort of the truth but with a better story. It'll make the story a little more interesting and more fun to tell, but it won't be true. I take less notice of him than I might a crow or a mockingbird setting down on one of those rusted skeletons. It's the nature of my world that people, even if they bring trouble, and they almost bring some kind of trouble on the Rez, are just one more drip in the monotony of exhaustion and pain that makes up my childhood.

The sad truth of it is that even him looking like some kind of monster, that strange limp, the way that he shuffles instead of walks, the wildness and woundedness of his appearance, isn't remarkable in this place. Bad nutrition and drink leave so many people looking that way. Some were born that way because their mothers or their fathers or both had drunk too much and eaten too little and everything that they did eat was made of sugar or corn or bleached white something. It's not all that unusual to see people without arms or legs because of diabetes or because they passed out drunk on the train tracks. Even with the money from casinos most of us don't take care of ourselves the way white people do. Maybe because we're still raised by people who got beat down by the kihnarà:ken, by the white people, till they believed their lives didn't matter.

I pretty much assume that the man's going to hurt me.

I mean I don't think he's a Wendigo or anything like that. Just something about him like he just gave up on being human. He's in jail again. My rake'níha. My father. I'm all alone except for Goat, and she's too old to do all that much damage to a stranger. I'm too small and skinny and weak to put up much of a fight.

I fight back most of the time anyway. I never seem to have the sense to sit still and just take it the way that other kids on the Rez have figured out to do, to just take it until it comes to a stop. I keep getting up until I can't get up anymore. I almost always make it worse.

I know that sooner or later someone's going to kill me.

Maybe I hope that sooner or later somebody will kill me.

I don't know.

I don't want much to be alive. I don't want much to be here. I just don't have the energy to kill myself. I've thought about all the different ways to do it but it's too much work.

It'd be so much easier if somebody kills me.

Maybe this strange monster looking limping man will be the one.

Even if he isn't a Wendigo. He's probably some kind of monster.

I don't honestly know any more if I actually want to die or if it's just not in me to lie down and stay down, that I'm just too stubborn to die.

The doctors say I'm going to die. But that's going to take a while.

And it's going to hurt.

A lot.

People keep saying I'm brave. I'm not brave.

My brain doesn't work the way it's supposed to. Even on the Rez people think I'm strange. Some of the older kids compare me to the character in that old movie Cool Hand Luke because they beat on me and I keep getting back up. I love that movie. I thought maybe it was meant as a kind of compliment. But later, when I watched that movie again, when I saw the sick look on the convicts' faces when Luke wouldn't stop getting up, couldn't stop getting up, even when he knew that he'd been licked by George Kennedy. I knew then it's not a compliment. I figure I might end up like Luke did at the end of that movie. Lying dead on a dirty floor with a big stupid grin on my face.

The beatings from him, from my rake'níha, from my father, and my mother when I see her, and strangers when I see them, are just one more tributary of the monotonous suffering that is the stinking river of my childhood. This monster looking man will probably hurt me and root through the house, the burned out ruin that passes for our home, my home, in search of something that he can take. He might even kill me.

I'm so dulled to pain, so tired, and the possibility of death that I can't even find a way to care about that.

I'll miss my Grandmother. And my friend, Roger. My only friend. He's older than me but he takes the time to teach me to fight and hunt. I don't know why. Probably pity.

I'll definitely miss Goat. She's as close to a good friend as I've got besides Roger.

And I guess I'll miss my cousin Dianne too. She checks in on me and brings me food. Probably because she feels like she has to. She's nice. She's pretty too.

I might miss them if there's some place you keep being after you die. But I won't miss my life. I won't miss waking up every single day weak and sick wondering out what bad thing will happen to me today.

If this bad thing will finally be the last bad thing that will ever happen, that wouldn't be so terrible.

He won't find anything in the house.

He sold or traded anything that mattered. My rake'níha. My father. He almost burned down the house and even when they gave him money to rebuild the house he spent it on booze and drugs and just left the house the way it was. They even gave him a trailer and he sold that. What he didn't sell or trade somebody else came and took. I buried some raccoon and squirrels that I caught. Deep down in a plastic bag with salt. Some nuts too. But he won't find any of it. I learned how to hide things so well that even a coyote or a badger couldn't find them. And Goat's a better guard dog than most dogs when it comes to that. If anyone gets too close to the house she'll raise a racket, even if she can't stop them.

She's raising one hell of a racket right now.

The monster man's head is down and his shoulders are hunched forward in a way that reminds me of the boxers that I saw when Roger took me to his gym. He doesn't look up. Not even once. No sign that he sees me, or even notices Goat, except that he's walking straight towards us. Every few steps he stops like he's lost and mutters to himself. Then he kind of sways, like he's struggling to get going again, and he keeps coming.

I just stand here leaning against the old fence post watching him.

I'm too tired to try getting away.

I could probably outrun him, slow as he is. But trying to get away just isn't worth the effort. Besides, running would only put off this particular bad thing. If he doesn't do something bad to me someone else will probably give me a beating today. Or tomorrow.

Maybe I just want it all to come to an end. I don't know.

Maybe I'm hoping this stranger, this strange scarred up hollow of a man, might be the one that finally finishes it.

He's close now. I can make out all the scars. There's a lot of them. All over his head and all over his face too. He mostly keeps his head down. I can see his hands and knuckles are all scarred up too, and I'm thinking maybe I was right about him being an old fighter.

Or maybe just someone who's as stupid and as stubborn as I am.

If I lived long enough I'd probably end up looking an awful lot like him.

I won't live that long.

Either way this stranger is probably dangerous.

Maybe he will be the one to finally end it.

He stops when he's about twenty feet away and looks at me, blinks, and then looks past me as if he doesn't actually see me. I'm used to that look. Lots of people look past me like that. Mostly just before they hurt me.

He looks around at the yard, at all the garbage and dirt and dried up patches of grass and then up at the sky and then down at the ground. Then he looks at Goat, which gets her raising even more of a racket. If she wasn't tied up she'd probably go after him.

She and I have got that in common.

It doesn't make much of a difference to either of us that we can't win the fight.

He just stands there for the longest time.

And I just stand there too.

Waiting.

Neither one of us looking at each other.

People don't look right at each other on the Rez anyway.

That's asking for a fight.

We stand there, watching what we can out of the corners of our eyes.

Even Goat gets quiet and just stands there.

Waiting.

I'm used to waiting.

I'm pretty good at waiting.

Waiting is one more thing you get used to on the Rez.

The stranger's face is all scars and lumps. One eye's so scarred over that it's barely open and both his ears are like raw cauliflower.

He doesn't look like an Indian.

But then again, neither do I.

Not really.

I've got dark hair and dark skin. It gets real dark in the summer and never burns. But there's enough of my mother in my features that those kids on the Rez who do look Indian, even though a lot of them have got less of the blood than I do, beat on me for not being Indian enough. And the kids in the city beat on me because I'm not white enough.

This guy's skin is pale. Not the kind of pale that looks natural. The kind of pale that comes from spending too much time inside.

Prison.

He gets that look when he's been in for a while. My rake'níha. My father.

The man doesn't have all the tattoos that most men who spend time in prison have got.

Men like him. My father. My rake'níha.

This guy looks like he can't remember what it's like to have freedom. He looks like he's used to being in a cage.

He has high cheekbones the kind of shape to his face that might make you think that he had Indian blood, but you would have to look closely to see it, or to see that he seems to know this place in a deep way, in the way that comes from growing up in a place like this.
We're not supposed to call it Indian.
I can't remember what we're supposed to call it now.
Kanien'keha:ka for our tribe.
But I can't remember for the rest of them.
- Much chance you got any water around, I suppose. - He doesn't say it like a question. More like a fact that he's already figured on.
His voice sounds tired. Dry and full of gravel. The tips of two of his fingers are nicotine stained. Like he smokes rolled up cigarettes instead of store bought.
- No. - I say. - I emptied the jug last night.
That's true. I would have said it to him even it wasn't, but I used up the last of the water and didn't get around to filling the jug back up yet.
The man stands there staring at the ground. He keeps his thumbs straight on the outside of his hands the way old boxers do. I'm starting to wish he'd get it over with. I also hope that he's not one of those that like little boys. I've had that tried on me a few times. They always start by telling me how pretty I am for a boy. Up until now I always managed to put up enough of a fight to make them decide that I wasn't worth all the trouble. I'm not expecting to get away with that forever. But I'm not looking forward to what happens when I don't.
- Didn't see no pump. - The man says. - Guessing that place of yours got no running water anymore.

Again it was more like he's stating what he's pretty sure is a fact than like he's asking a question.

I think for a moment about lying about where he is. Where my rake'níha is.

But it doesn't seem worth all the effort. He won't take long to find out that I'm all alone if that's what he wants.

- There's a creek back in the woods. - I say - I usually get my water from there.

I don't know why I said that. I know better than to give anything to a stranger. Even information. Giving anything away that you don't have to never works out for anything but bad on the Rez.

- It ain't too clean. - I say.

We stand there for a little while.

I'm already getting bored.

Mostly people hurting each other is just one more way of not being bored in this place.

I figure he's coming due to hurt me soon though.

He just stands there though. Looks around. Looks up at the sky. Then back down at the ground.

It seems to me like he does that a lot.

- I don't have money. - He says - Don't... Don't have too much of nothin.

He shuffles his feet. Something in the way he's standing there gives me the feeling that he isn't going to hurt me.

But I know better than to trust anything in this place.

Or maybe I just hope that he's going to turn out to be a lot worse than he's looking right now.

- Don't suppose you could point me to the creek. - He says - I can't give you anything for it.

Despite all the scars and the look of somebody who spent a lot of time in prison, there's something about him that feels kind of gentle. Not kind maybe. And not towards everybody. But towards me and those like me. And he doesn't talk like most of the people on the Rez or any of the bad ones who spend most of their time in jail.

He isn't going to hurt me.

Because I'm just a boy. Maybe because I can't hurt him.

- I could bring you there I suppose. - I'm as surprised at having said it as he seems to be at my having said it.

He looks straight at me for just a brief moment, as if he was seeing me for the first time and then looks back down at the ground.

We stand there for a while just not looking at each other.

I can tell he isn't going to hurt me. There's violence in him. A whole lot of rage and violence. He still seems very dangerous. Even with all the damage I can see that's been done to him, he still seems like someone who can take care of himself in a pinch. That violence is probably not going to be turned on me. He would probably never use it on someone like me.

I still don't trust him.

I don't trust anybody.

That part of me that won't and can't believe that even the people who have been good to me, won't hurt me sooner or later. Maybe he would never hurt someone like me. I still can only see being hurt as something not very important, and not being hurt as a kind of disappointment.

Maybe I'm a little bit sorry that it's not going to end for me today.

He licks his lips, and the sound that his lips and his mouth make when he does that tells me that he has gone without water and been in the hot sun for way too long.

- If you don't want me to take you. - I say. - That's fine too.

I want him to know that I don't care one way or the other.

I don't care one way or the other.

But I want him to know that I don't.

He licks his lips again. They're dry and chapped, and the inside of his mouth sounds dry and chapped. I can hear it from where I am.

- If it won't be too much trouble. - He says - I guess I'm pretty thirsty and I could use some water. If that won't be too much trouble.

I shrug my shoulders.

Then I turn and start to head towards the creek.

I stop when I realize that he isn't following. He's just standing there with this lost look on his face, like he's confused or just can't figure out if he wants the water after all.

- Mister. - I say - This is the way if you want some water.

He gives me a kind of startled look and then looks back down at the ground and nods his head. The gesture's so small and so slight that I barely see it. - Don't you want to grab your jug? - He asks me.

This time a real question.

I stare at him. Then I go into the house and get my jug.

Goat looks at me when I come back out.

I go over and untie her.

- She won't hurt you. - I say to the man. Just in case he's scared of goats. Some people are. - She needs water too.

I lead them down to the creek.

The monster man follows me with that strange shuffling limp of his.

I'm not all that sure he'll be able to make it to the creek.

And I'm not all that sure, if he doesn't make it, if I'll try to help him make it or not.

I'm not sure if I care one way or the other.

Moccasin Face

I have floated through time and from body to body for as long as there has been time and the bodies from which to count that time. I have seen and done many things through many different eyes and always I am able to pass for one of them.
I know the exquisite silence of death.
I have grown fond of death.
Perhaps because I can never truly know death. Or perhaps because I love the empty and dark silence that always follows death.
I take joy in bringing death to others.
I have lost count of how many deaths that I have brought.
It has been so many.
I like to watch the life slipping from behind their eyes and I like to watch their spirits leave the flesh behind to wander lost and suffering for the rest of what it is that they have come to call time.
In this body I have killed over a hundred I think.
Some have said that it is more than one hundred and fifty. Others that it is a little as one hundred. Still others have said that it might be more than two hundred.
I have lost count.
The exact number does not matter to me.
Numbers seem to matter very much to them. But I do not care.
Though there have been moments where I have tried to count how many lives I have taken in each body so that I know if it is more or less than in the past. I have always grown tired of trying to count.

I do not think that this body has killed over one hundred and fifty.

Most were men. Some were women and children.

I have no particular care about who it is that I kill. One sack of meat is pretty much like the other. It is the exquisite silence of death that I long for and that I kill for and in my opinion they all make too much noise in the coming to the silence.

His enemies calls this body Two Stick because he wields a war club in each hand during battle.

The people of his village call him Moccasin Face because his face resembles a worn out moccasin that has been stitched together again and again.

They do not call him that to his face.

But I have heard them say it just the same.

I do not care what any of them call him. Just so long as he is permitted to kill.

That is all that I have ever cared about.

Before there were these two leg creatures I have been here. There were other creatures then. But the two legs are the best to be and to kill because they are aware of death and afraid of death and their minds are filled with hatred and fear and ridiculous reasons to kill that have nothing to do with any real need to kill at all and they are best to kill because they make so much more noise than any of the other living things and thus the silence is so sweet.

It is fun to be Moccasin Face.

There is so much talk to hear about the side that he belongs to and the ones that he does not belong to, about his tribe against that tribe, about good people and bad people. But in the end it always comes down to yet another reason for the killing and that brings me such pleasure. I do not care about the reasons, but the lies that hide behind them make these two legs so much more interesting and so much more fun than other creatures.

They are happy to have him use his war clubs on their enemies.

They are even happy that he brings their enemies' great pain.

They just do not want to know that he enjoys it.

They do not want to know that I enjoy it.

They just do not want to know or to believe how very much that I enjoy the killing.

They want him to enjoy the fight. They want him to enjoy the battle.

They would not be pleased to realize that we enjoy the killing.

That would shatter their carefully constructed illusions. And there is no greater sin that you can commit among these two legs than to rupture their layers of crusted lies.

They would not even like to know how much pleasure I take in the killing of the Black Robes.

The Black Robes, who stink worse than a bear coming out of its winter sleep, whose skin is so pale that they look sickly even when sun lingers, and who speak a language that is as awful as their smell.

The Black Robes who want to force a new God on these people. A God who will not accept any of the other Gods because his ego is so large. Who has rules that the Black Robes speak but do not live.

The Black Robes who bring sickness and bad medicine from across the great water on their big boats but who cannot even paddle a canoe in the gentlest parts of the great river. Who want to give that river the name of one of their sainted medicine man from a world they come from, a name that has nothing to do with this river or with this world. Who do not even know the river but think that they can give it a name of their own.

They are delicious, these Black Robes.

They lie to themselves more beautifully than any I have seen before this.

But even these self-righteous creatures I am not supposed to take pleasure in killing.

The Black Robes mostly avoid Moccasin Face. The Black Robes mostly avoid me. Something in them sees what I am and they know without knowing to keep their distance from me though that often does not do them any good in the end.

Most of the women avoid Moccasin Face too.

His face is too ugly and too frightening and perhaps they too see in his eyes that I would enjoy hurting them if given the chance to do so.

I am happy to be left alone to my own musings, and to my own special pleasures. Though I would love to catch one of these Black Robes alone.

The Wyandot have grown so sick with these Black Robes' disease that their people are fewer now than Moccasin Face's, even though they were once a much larger Nation than Moccasin Face's tribe ever was.

That is the disappointing thing that the Black Robes have done.

They have killed more Wyandot than even I could ever kill.

But many of his people, particularly the women and children have also taken to the Black Robes' teachings and have been felled by their bad Medicine. They kneel and pray before this new tortured God even as they die from the Black Robe demons and their wonderfully terrible diseases.

And the Black Robes call the Wyandot, their allies, Huron. An insult. Their insult their own allies.

I would like to kill all the Black Robes if I could, but they are so deliciously murderous and duplicitous in their own right that it seems almost a shame to kill them at all.

I would like to kill all the pale devils who come across the Great Water, but they bring their Bad Medicine and their selfish insecure God with them and I so enjoy watching them destroy even the souls of the people that they claim that they wish to save. I like watching the destruction that they bring. I would like to poke a hole in their guts and slowly pull their entrails out while boiling their lower bodies and their scrotums in scalding water or to hang them upside down over a small slow fire to bake the inside of their heads ever so slowly just to watching them scream and denounce their jealous God. But they do such delicious harm, and the Elders of his Council have spoken, and said that he should not kill them or do things to them until they give him good reason.

The pale two legs' Algonquin guides call Moccasin Face's people Man-eaters. The Algonquins themselves have been known to eat parts of men in order to send them into the next world without their best and strongest parts. The Algonquin live in dirt huts like Beavers and run away from his people rather than stand and fight. The Algonquin help the pasty skinned two legs that have crossed great waters to claim the land and banish old Gods and who understand nothing of this world yet think that they can tell those already here how to live and put names on things that they do know.

Moccasin Face has killed many Algonquin.

He has eaten parts of their bodies.

I have eaten parts of their bodies.

The Algonquin are far stronger and braver than the Black Robes who look down on even them.

Moccasin Face once caught a white skinned soldier in the woods. The soldier tried to aim his thunder stick at Moccasin Face, but it was raining, and they seem only able to call upon the thunder when the sky is not using it. I could see the fear in the soldier's eyes even though he was supposed to be one of their warriors. I cut thin strips off the soles of his feet and he screamed like a frightened rabbit. I cut a hole in his belly and dragged some of his innards out. He screamed and cried and he begged Moccasin Face. I could not understand his words but I knew the begging for what it was. Then Moccasin Face took his knife and dug holes in both sides of the soldier's mouth, and he pried out his teeth out through the holes in the man's cheeks one by one. The soldier cried in ways that even children would not cry and I thought if this is what the white skinned warriors are, then the Black Robes, who will not even fight, must be weaker than anyone can even imagine. The soldier soiled himself and vomited and urinated all over the insides of his clothes. The smell was a wonderful thing. Crows came along and I let them have their way with him after cutting out his tongue and feeding it to the crows so that he could not scream out loud anymore. His screams were growing tiresome even for me.

But he broke so very deeply and quivered with so much fear and weakness that it filled me with bliss.

I did not eat any part of him.

I was so deeply thankful for his cowardice and his weakness but I feared having it inside Moccasin Face's body, for fear that that weakness might enter me.

I decided then and there that these creatures with skin the colour of the underbelly of a toad and their hairy faces were the very best ones to kill. I hope that many more of them will come over the great water and bring their weakness and their one delusional God with them.

Oh, it would please me so.

I was beginning to despair that these stoic people in Moccasin Face's world would never give me the kind of pleasure that I most deeply desired.

These creatures walk and move like the other two legs. They resemble the other two legs except for their pale skin and all the hair on their faces and bodies. But they are something much better. They are something far more precious than those that were already here, because they have such great delusions and so little courage. They fill me with happiness with the weak ways that they die and the diseases and destruction that they leave behind them.

Even the Wyandot, even the dirt dwelling Algonquin have showed more strength, more dignity and more courage than these hairy, sickly pale, soft and cowardly creatures.

I have resolved that the next time that Moccasin Face catches one of these creatures I will cut him open little by little, to try to keep him alive for as long as possible so that I can see if their insides work in the same way that other two legs do.

Perhaps they are not even of the same world.

Perhaps they do not work in the same way at all.
I do not know if cutting them open will reveal their secrets.
It probably will not.
It can be very tricky to tell the insides of one thing from another sometimes.
But at the very least I will cause the next one as much pain as possible before killing them.
That is one thing that I enjoy even more than the killing.
That is the one thing that I have made Moccasin Face better at even than killing.
He will cause them such incredible pain.
He will cause them such great and truly terrible pain.
And I will enjoy every delicious moment of it.
I will enjoy that next time the most, I think.
I think that I will enjoy the next one more than any of the others so far.
Especially if the next one is one of the wonderful pale skins.

Dianne

Her name was Eliza.

Eliza Darquisse Dumont.

But everyone called her Dianne, and nobody knew why.

Nobody, including Dianne, could remember why.

She was a pretty young woman, Dianne. And, while she had many suitors, she had no intention of becoming anyone's wife or anyone's mother. Not if she could help it. Olive coloured skin dabbed here and there with soft freckles and high cheekbones and shimmering black hair with copper streaks that reflected the sunlight on clear days. Her eyes were ever so slightly almond shaped and the colour of almonds too, which led some to speculate that she might have Oriental blood in her.

Oriental.

That's what they called it then.

It was an obliquely musical and distant word for something that the people in that place could only understand within a very uncertain frame. There was only one Chinese family and their take-out food place, some half remembered thoughts of Marco Polo or Genghis Khan or Bruce Lee.

It raised her in their eyes above the Indian heritage about which she would never tell them.

For the people in that place knew Indians, that's what they called them then, all too well. They knew about the people who lived on the Island, who were not even good enough to be white trash. People who they feared and resented because they were as close to the absolute and despised Other as anyone in that place could know. There was no black family there then. Italians to them were not white and Jews almost certainly ate babies and had killed Jesus.

Dianne was kind and gentle. She was pretty and she was decent. She couldn't possibly be Indian.

Being kind and decent was an unusual thing then in that place. While our memories haze and soften our past into the "good old days", there never truly was such a thing. At least not where Dianne grew up. Her goodness was most unusual coming from the family that she did, the one she would never tell anyone about.

She had been raised away from her brothers and sisters and her parents, part of the government scoop that took children away from Native families and placed them with white families for their own good.

That's what the government said.

That's what the government called it then.

A kindness.

As the youngest girl, she could not be sent into the woods to hide the way her other siblings had, and she had been found and taken. She had been taken in by good and decent white parents, and afforded a kind of luxury living away from that Island, of having and being able to keep her gentler instincts. It seemed then like a good bargain for giving up her past and her culture, especially since the church told her again and again that Indians were heathen Satan worshippers who had murdered and tortured priests.

Dianne tried to be kind to the boy.

She knew that the boy lived an especially hard life, that he had suffered untold and unknown abuses that he would never speak of. Not to her and not to anyone else. She felt deep in her soul that he was meant to be a good boy and she believed that his cold and brittle distance from her and all the rest of humanity was a kind of armour, a kind of shield wall that the boy had created to protect himself from the ugly world of the Reserve, which was the only world that he had never known.

Dianne knew these things to be true without the words ever having to be spoken.

Some things have a truth to them that runs far deeper than the shallow surface skimmed by spoken words.

She had thought of perhaps adopting the boy, of taking him away from the Island, of taking him away from that world the way that she had been taken, but she feared the boy's father. She knew the boy's father. She had seen the look in his eyes when he was drunk and angry. And he was always drunk and angry. Dianne knew that the father was capable of terrible things. And she knew that the boy's father was not the only threat to him on that Island.

That was another truth that ran far deeper than words that could be spoken.

Dianne was not at all certain that the boy would even be willing to go.

She did not pretend, even to herself, to understand the boy.

She could only do her best to love him.

She brought the boy food and clothing when she could, to that half burned down house. But she was always careful that none of her friends or anyone from her life could see her crossing the river. Most of them did not know Dianne/ Eliza Darquisse Dumont's connection to that Island. And she was not ready for them to know about that connection. She did not know if she would ever be ready for that.

The boy never seemed to wear the clothes that she brought him, and he would wolf down the food without ever taking the time to taste it or to show any appreciation for what Dianne did for him. She did not know what happened to the clothes.

Some of them surely, along with much of the food, were eaten by his goat. That boy would give the goat food even when he himself was starving.

He would not tell her about these things if she asked.

She never asked.

But she knew.

Mostly, she knew.

He was a strange and sickly boy. She did not think that this was solely due to his terrible life or even to the living of a cruel and terrible life. He was very smart. His grades were very good despite his sporadic attendance, and she believed him to be a good boy, though he showed little evidence of that, other than that he did not seem to do particularly bad things, the kinds of bad things that Dianne knew that boys and men and women and even girls did on that Reserve, the kinds of bad things that the boy's family was known to do, because that was all that any of them knew.

His Grandmother said that the boy could see things that most others could not see, that he could hear things that most others could not hear. The Grandmother said that the boy had Strong Power, Ka'shatsténhshera'kó:wa, she said, the same kind of power as she, his Grandmother was said to have. But Dianne had been raised a good Catholic girl and she did believe in such things.

Not really.

Still she loved the boy.

Still she tried to as kind to him as she felt that she was allowed to be.

She did not like going to that Island.

They had money on the Reserve now, Casino money, and they had cleaned most of the place up, but that Island still felt to Dianne like a terrible savage and cruel thing. She could feel the ghosts of cruelty that still lingered there in that place in her good Catholic bones. It was a place where people like the boy's Grandmother believed in things that would surely send them all to hell, and where, even now, with all the money and the new houses and new boats, terrible things, things that had been done to people for generations, were still done. She knew that the boy believed in some of the old ways, some of the Wild ways, but he also read the Bible and knew it better than most people who called themselves Christians, even though he was just a boy. And Dianne believed, she wanted dearly to believe that the boy would come to the good Catholic God in his own way and in his own time.

She would not tell him what to believe.

He would not listen if she did tell him.

Dianne knew what it was to be told what to believe and what it meant to people on that Island to be told what to believe and what not to believe, and she knew about the horrible things that were done through the centuries to make the people believe in a thing that they did not want to believe. She was not naive. She was not a fool. She knew what horrible things had been done to people in the name of God and in the name of civilization. She knew what had been done to the boy's Grandmother and Grandfather and all the Grandparents that were from that place by her own Catholic Church.

Dianne believed nonetheless in the overall goodness of the Church in the same way that she believed the overall goodness of the boy.

But she had also come to believe that a person should arrive at the things that they believed because they chose to believe in that thing, not because someone else had decided for them that they should believe it.

Many at Dianne's Church would not agree with that idea. Dianne never spoke it out loud.

She did her very best to be a good woman, did Dianne/ Eliza Darquisse Dumont, and she succeeded at it better than most.

But still she worried that the things that the things that the boy's Grandmother believed, and that the boy himself seemed to believe at times, would send the boy to hell. And Dianne did not want that for the boy.

Not for him.

She went out there to the Island when she could.

On that day she went to bring the boy food.

Dianne knew that the boy had been taught to hunt and trap in the old ways and that he hid food somewhere so that he would have it if she did not come, but he was just a boy and the things that he could hunt and trap could not possibly be enough to sustain him, and nothing grew in the ground on that Island because of the years of chemicals being spilled into the river and the food that he hid could go bad and kill him. He was so sick, so thin and gaunt and fragile looking already. She feared that one day she would come to the Island and find him dead of starvation or poisoning or of the violence that was still so much a part of that unchristian and savage place.

There were churches on the Reserve. There were Christians. And those that weren't were not all savage and cruel.

Dianne knew this to be true.

But it was a violent world. More violent even than the outside world, the world that Dianne knew. And the violence seemed to hang over the boy like a dark brooding cloud that might strike him down with lightning and thunder and mindless cruelty at any moment.

Dianne felt deeply the boy's loss even though it had not yet happened.

She felt how a gaping emptiness would be left in the world where this boy once was.

In her heart.

And in the world itself.

But she felt that his loss was inevitable, like the falling of the leaves and then the falling of the snow and then the falling of the rains that are separated by a too brief sunlight.

Dianne/Eliza felt an aching for the boy and for the brittle useless armour that this too often cruel world, a world as a whole that was cruel by default, let alone the world of the island where violence could come so quickly and without warning, as much out of sheer boredom and not knowing of anything else as because it was just easier to pass on the hurt, had forced him to hide behind, the shield wall of not caring and of never being truly there, or in any place at all, so that when this too was taken from him he could tell himself that it had never truly mattered anyway, that he had never truly mattered anyway.

Dianne did not let the boy see, not ever, that she pitied him, that she feared for him or even that she loved the boy. She knew that such things were alien to him and that he would retreat from any sign of emotion further behind his brittle shield wall, perhaps so far behind it that she could never reach him again.

She brought him food and sometimes clothing that he would never wear, and she let him have his distance. She did not try to reach beyond the wall or beyond his distance.
But she did love the boy.
She did not understand him.
She did not even really know the boy but she did nonetheless love him.
That day, as she pulled her almost paid for car up the gravel driveway that was blotched and spattered with weeds and garbage in front of the half burned down house that looked like it might fall from rot and neglect at any moment, she did not see the boy. Usually, if he was here he would be standing outside, by the burned post. He stood there most often, eyes far, so far away. as if he was in some kind of trance.
Just him and the goat.
He spent very little time inside the house.
He spent very little time inside at all.
The cockroaches and the ants and the flies and the rats had the run of the inside of that house which still stank of fire and filth.
It was not unusual for the boy not be there.
But the goat was not there either.
He often went out to hunt or trap and he sometimes went on long walks that could last for days. Walks that the boy's Grandmother said was an old sacred practice, a kind of communion with spirits. But Dianne suspected that the boy just walked to get away, to get away from the ugly and unkind thing that was his life.
The first few times he had done it Dianne had feared for the boy's life. He went with no food or water and days without

sleep, often so deep into the woods that no one could have found him, and he was just a boy, so small and frail and sickly. She feared that he would not find his way home or that he had no intention of finding his way home. But he always came back. And she began to learn not to fear for the boy quite so much when he disappeared on those walks.

Dianne got out of the car and grabbed her bags of food.

They had agreed on a place that she could leave food where it wouldn't be found or stolen to easily, or torn into by the rats or the local dogs or coyotes. Or the goat that ate everything and seemed to hate the world even more than the boy. The food would probably still be there if he had gone on a walk, when he got back.

As she walked towards the house that still stank of fire, Dianne's thoughts were on the things that would make up the remainder of her day. The drive back and the visits to friends and neighbours that took up so much of her days off.

It was a long moment before she finally too notice of the boy, the goat and a strange man walking away from her across the junk strewn field. She had been looking straight at them, but had been too lost in her own thoughts to see what it was that she was looking at.

The man. The stranger.

Dianne knew right away that she did not know this man and that he was not someone she had ever seen on the Island or anywhere on the Reserve, though she did not know how exactly it was that she was so certain of that. The way that the man walked, the strange limping shuffling gait and the hunched over way that he carried his body filled Dianne with immediate and terrible dread.

Dianne had, in her nightmares, seen a stranger like this one come for the boy. She had always feared that some stranger, some unknown faceless predator would come for the boy while his father was in prison and while Dianne was away, and the nightmares always ended with the boy's body in a field very much like the one that he and the man were now walking across, the body mutilated and violated beyond all redemption or human capacity for understanding by some faceless nameless human monster.

Dianne/Eliza Darquisse Dumont froze where she was, in mid step, and opened her mouth to scream.

But no sound came out.

The faceless hunched over man and the goat and the boy continued to walk away from her in that barren rusted out field and Dianne/Eliza Darquisse Dumont could not move or make any sound.

The bags slipped from her numb hands and cans rolled and food splattered all over the dirty gravelled driveway.

And Dianne screamed without making the slightest sound.

While the boy, the goat and the man moved further and further away.

Dianne/Eliza Darquisse Dumont screamed and screamed and screamed.

And no sound came out.

Not the slightest sound came out her mouth.

Not the slightest sound.

Still she continued to scream into that terrible silence.

Faller

call me faller.
what they called me.
what they call me now.
what i call myself most of the time.
i call myself faller and they call me faller because that's what i am. that's who i am.
the worst insult you can hear if you're a fighter. the worst insult you can ever hear. worse than bastard or sonofabitch or coward or cocksucker.
mostly they don't say it to my face.
mostly.
not at first but they said it and i heard it. and i didn't say nothing. and i say it myself now. because it's what i am.
i could fight.
i still can fight.
mostly.
i could win most of those fights. i can't remember when exactly i stopped knowing i could win. i can't remember anything exactly right no more. but the first time that somebody offered me money and i took it. and then i kept taking it because taking it was easy. the money. a lot easier than not knowing how the fight was going to turn out. a lot easier after a while than saying i didn't want to take the money no more. the thing is after a while i didn't even need to fake it. after a while i started to fall down for real. even though i used to be able to take any punch or kick and stay on my feet. all of a sudden i couldn't. and even the maybe. even the maybe of being a halfway good fighter was gone.

they used to call it punchy.
when your brain gets all scrambled from too many hits.
punchy. hands started to shake. the world started to look
like broken television. i couldn't remember things even
simple things. people started to sound like they were talking
from another room even when they were right there.
and i started falling down all on my own.
i would be walking along. the next thing i knew somebody
was looking down at me. i was looking up at them. or at the
ceiling. or up at the sky. the doctors even the bad ones even
the very worst ones wouldn't pass me to fight. not even in
the dive bars no more. i was washed up. the booze and the
drugs that were always part of it. then that's all there was.
wasn't even the fighting. i wasn't even anything like a real
fighter. not even the maybe of being a real fighter. i started
to steal and rob. acting crazy. even crazier than i ever was.
all the time in the joint. like i was in more than i was out.
the doctors in the joint telling me about scar tissue on my
brain. making me fall down. all the tests. more tests that i
couldn't even say the name of. my brain didn't work right.
maybe it never did work right. but now it was really fucked
up. all i wanted to do was get out. just get out. get wasted
and drunk to forget the pain. forget i was a useless drunk.
useless drugged up fuck. washed up. all washed up.
then i started to think about going back.
started to think all the time about going back to the river.
nothing but the river. no plans. no ideas except the river
and going back.
every time i got out i would do something crazy end up back
in the joint. get back on the booze. get back on the drugs.
crack mostly. any kind of drugs i could get my hands on.

anything to make the darkness not so heavy. make the darkness not so smothering for a little while. i would need more money. so i would do something stupid. get caught. end right back in the joint again. i never was no criminal genius. just some idiot that wanted something to push the darkness back just a little bit.

sometimes i would still get a fight for money. even then. it wouldn't take more than one good shot before i was falling down again. the money got less. even less every single time. the fights got uglier. i got uglier. uglier meaner places. i got meaner. got easier to rob some place or break into some place. i was never smart enough to get that right. end up back inside. all i could think about was needing to get back to the river. only way the story could end. all i wanted. the fucking story to end.

i didn't have no more feeling about dying than i did about living. just needed to get to the river.

to the end. it needed to fit somehow. the beginning to the end. i was born dead. the actual dying was just some word. a word that was way past the time to say it.

just needed to stay out for even a minute. so i could make it back to the river.

but i needed money. every time i tried to get my hands on cash. just ended up back inside. social workers. bible thumpers. telling me they could get me money from the government. on account of my head being so messed up. but i didn't want the government's money. just wanted my own money. all i needed some halfway decent score where i didn't get caught. except i was never smart enough not to get caught. not even before all the head damage.

the one social worker. fat and pasty. like a slug. lizard eyes.

got real pissed at me because i didn't want the government's money. that i would steal it from some store owner who never did nothing to me. that fat lizard eye slob couldn't figure that. stealing wasn't begging or taking handouts. didn't even bother trying to tell it to him. it would never make no sense to someone like him. taking money from the government to go around like he gave a shit.
i got out and saw him on the street one day and kicked his fat slug lizard face in.
kicked it in so bad he died.
the lawyer brings up my head damage. said some shit about the guy diddling prisoners. i get seven for manslaughter.
when i got out this time i just started walking. kept on walking. no money. nothing to sleep in. just clothes and shoes. shoes worn through with holes. i got to the river. to the place where the river got started. or ended. i can never remember which one. i just kept on walking. i didn't know where exactly. to the island. to the rez. didn't know where the house where i grew up even was. where it used to be. just hoped that if i kept on walking i might come to the place. if there was a real place that i remembered. i would know it. i would know that place. then it could all be just end. i didn't give a shit about them coming after me anymore. i just wanted to get to get to the river. get all the fucked up shit to end. all the falling down and all the other shit to end finally. just get to the river. to the island. where it started so i could get it to end.
i never did find the place. maybe because it was all twisted. maybe because i was all changed. maybe because i couldn't find the memories no more. with all the getting hit in the head and the falling down. i kept walking thinking maybe

i would run into some place i would know. even without remembering it. but the rez was changed. not the dead filthy stinking thing i remembered. something cleaner. almost pretty and soft. nothing i knew belonged there. i didn't belong there. they cleaned up all the memories. scrubbed them clean. so clean they didn't even belong to me no more. this wasn't my world no more. i could walk forever and nothing was going to be my remembering of it.

it was that knowing. that the island wasn't the place from my memories. it left me all of a sudden worn out. tired. hot. dry in my mouth so i couldn't even swallow or make spit. long time ago i would go off into the woods without food or water. i would walk without sleeping or stopping. old woman told everybody i was doing some kind of spirit walk. all i was doing was walking. getting away from the world. getting away from the old man's fists. sometimes i think maybe i was doing some kind of spirit walk. i just didn't know it. like the old lady was telling the truth without me knowing it was the truth.

mostly i was just walking.

i was feeling like i couldn't walk no more. then i see the boy. this skinny kid standing there watching me. arms wrapped around burned out old fence post. half burned down house. old goat tied up with a rope. he felt to me like i knew him. the kid i mean. like he was something or somebody. that half burned down house and the goat. like i knew it. like i remembered it.

i felt like i knew the kid. and like maybe he would know me. crazy.

so i started walking to them.

i didn't even don't even know why i was walking.

i didn't even know right away i was walking.
somehow my feet changed direction without my knowing
it. i was walking to this boy that i didn't know. his old goat
i didn't know. but i was sure i knew them.
the kid didn't move.
just stood there.
the goat was raising a racket. but then even the goat got
quiet. like it knew me.
crazy. batshit crazy.
in that place. probably still even behind all the nice houses
and the shiny boats. for a kid to just stand there when a grown
up especially a fucked up grown up was coming towards
him wasn't normal. i remembered that. i knew that. people
in that place were dangerous. even with more money in
pockets they were probably still dangerous. people in every
place are dangerous. but in a different way than in places like
that. in other places you don't know the kind of hurt they're
going to do. they don't mean no harm at first. but in in places
like the island the rez doing bad things is all there is. always
there underneath the clean and shiny outside. pretty much
anybody in that place still meant hurt. normal thing to do
is get out of the way or do something ugly before they do
something ugly to you.
the kid just stood there.
the goat just stood there.
he didn't look like there was nothing wrong with him. the
kid i mean. he didn't look like a retard. like he was off his
head. at least on the outside on the outside he looked normal.
but it wasn't normal in that place to just stand there. it was
not normal when you saw somebody fucked up like me.
scarred up and twitchy like me.

all the scars and the gimped up walk coming towards you.
but the kid just stood there and the goat just stood there.
they just stood there.
i kept on walking.
that's what happened.
just that.
just that.
them standing there and me walking to them.
that was the start.
not the end.
not the end yet.
almost maybe.
wherever i was going this was the start
i didn't even know where i was but that was the start.
i was done walking.
for now.
for now i was done walking.

The River

The River used to be a mighty thing.
The River used to be a killer of man and beast.
Coming down from the icy north with its brutal cold
and deadly current.
This River broke ships.
This River once tore canoes and men to pieces.
It left men shattered and crushed upon the rocks
of its mighty rapids.
It was a River to be feared.
It was a River to be respected.
It was a River to be thought of with awe.
Then they came in with bulldozers and blueprints and
they turned the River into something
that they could manage.
They turned this River into something that they could use
and they could feel safe around.
Just like they did with the bear,
they trapped the River's spirit.
They made its waters filthy with chemicals and sewage
from passing ships from all over the world, and its waters
stank and turned black and got clogged
with seaweed and garbage.
They caged the River.
They put the River in a hole.
They dug holes and they filled them with concrete and put
the River in those holes like they did with the bear,
and they left the River to die.
And before long they had no more use for the river.
There were fewer ships.

People and things were moved faster and easier by planes
and cheaper by trains and the thing that they had made
and called a river was no longer necessary.
Just this caged and filthy thing that they still called a river.
But this time some people got together and
they cleaned up the river.
Not all people are the same.
Not all people are bad.
Most of them want what's good and right,
but far too many of them settle for what's easy.
Some of the people, the ones who weren't willing to settle,
got together and they cleaned up as much of the sewage
and the filth as they could because it was making so many
of them sick. Because they could not bury the stink of the
river the way that they had buried the dead bear.
These people, they brought the river back
to something like life.
They did not give it back its Power, its Ka'shatsténhshera.
The river still could kill men, but only in the way that all
rivers and all water can kill men, by drowning them.
It could no longer break them.
It could no longer break ships or even canoes.
It could not long shatter the things that
men have made upon its rocks.
But they did make it beautiful again.
Now the river glitters like a painting in the sunlight and it
flows as softly and as gently as a painter's brush.
But that is all that people can see.
That is only the river's surface.
That is only the perfect face of what
they now call the river.
It is a tame thing now.

And, like all tame things it no longer inspires
the supernatural awe that it did when it was wild.
And, like all tame things, it is polluted,
just not in the obvious ways.
The river is still sick.
Just not in a way that you have to look at.
Just not in a way that you have to smell.
The river is not wild and it does not
cause nightmares anymore.
The rot is all beneath its surface now.
The poison is not where you can see it
or smell it or take any notice of.
But nothing that has been caged is healthy.
No thing that has been locked up can fully breathe.
And no thing that has been caged can be truly alive.
No matter how much we pretend that it is so.
No matter how pretty that we make it look.
The river is not truly alive.
Underneath its pretty face...
It is a dead thing.
It is a dead thing that is rotting.
Slowly surely rotting.
Yet now it's so pretty.
Now it's so very pretty.
Not mighty.
Not to be feared.
Not a River.
But so very pretty.

Killer

i killed another one.

i promised myself no more kids no more children but another one's dead and i killed her.

i lost count of how many now even if i try to add up just boys or girls the indians just the indigenous ones or the minorities or the white kids that no one would miss.

so many.

i keep expecting to get caught but the thing is that i'm so good at killing. i'm so well hidden that they'll probably never catch me they don't even know that these kids are being murdered just another kid that no one's going to miss.

then there's the women.

i haven't killed a woman in while but there's a lot of them mostly indians no one ever misses indians they go missing all the time.

indigenous women.

i'm just ending their misery.

same goes for the kids but the kids are a sickness in me and i try not to kill any more kids but i just keep killing them and getting away with it.

it's a sickness.

this little girl she didn't even cry or beg. the indian kids almost never cry or beg it's like they just figure they deserve it.

it's like they know they don't matter.

all the things i did to her she didn't cry out she barely made a sound it took so long for her to die i made her suffer i mean really suffer and not a sound not once did she beg me to stop.

they're tough those indian kids.
indigenous.
probably did her a favour.
still the kids are a sickness something i have to do and that's
how they all get caught indulging that's when you leave a
signature because you have to do it and sooner or later if
i keep doing what i have to do i'm definitely going to get
caught.
sometimes i think maybe i want to see how much i can get
away with how far i can go before they finally figure it out
but they're all so blind they don't think past what they see
on the surface and i know just how to do it but everyone
makes mistakes that's what they say at least but i haven't
made one big enough to get caught yet.
it's like i was born to do it.
if only they knew.
if all those people who think they know me found out what
it is i do what i really do who i really am.
this is who i am.
predator.
killer
a killer of children a killer of women.
the bogeyman that makes children who makes women
disappear.
a monster who lurks in the darkness right in front of them
who lurks in the places that they never look who brings
horrible suffering to the innocent and the not so innocent
who feeds on their pain and fear and suffering.
that is who i am.
that is what i am.
a child killer.

a woman killer.

an indian killer.

you're not supposed to call them indians anymore. i can't keep track. back in the day we were all okay with indians. when they were all drunks and indians. back then killing them would probably be okay with a lot of people.

back in my father's day.

when he was clearing the graves off the old residential school for the priests.

now we're supposed to feel guilty about what we did to them.

not even we.

some people back long time ago.

the priests and the politicians and the nuns.

we're supposed to feel guilty about what those people did. that took their land. that took their culture. that stuck them in residential schools and cut off their beautiful hair and tortured them until they didn't know they were indian anymore until they didn't know anymore what they're supposed to be.

not good enough to be white.

not even good enough to be black.

i would have had a good time back in those days.

those good old days.

nowadays you have to be careful about every word that comes out of your mouth and you can't keep track of what you're supposed to be calling things.

next week they'll want to be called indians again.

she had such beautiful eyes. the little girl. so many of those indian kids start out looking so beautiful. those big dark eyes. that hair that gleams black in the sun. it was a shame

to spoil all that beauty but life would have done it to her
sooner or later.
i did her a favour.
now she'll be beautiful forever.
well.
some of those indians believe you go into the next life
looking like you did when you died. if that's true then i
didn't do her any favours. she was definitely not beautiful
when i was done with her.
she just stared at me with those beautiful eyes. there was
fear there and plenty of pain but mostly she just looked
confused like she didn't know why this was happening to
her. not a sound. not a peep. but those eyes.
that made it all worthwhile.
i was ready if she tried to scream. i'm always ready. but i
like it so much better when they don't. maybe that's why i
like the indians most.
maybe.
or maybe because it's such a challenge to get them to scream
and i keep hoping i can make them scream.
or maybe it's just because no one will miss them. not anyone
that matters. the family might go to the police. they probably
will. and the police will write a report that just sits there.
nobody that matters cares about the indian ones.
the indigenous ones.
at first i thought it'd be a bigger deal but kids on the
reservation run away so often people just disappear so often
that police just can't be bothered to really look for them.
they might go talk to a few people but mostly they just file
the report and forget about it. even the police that care at
first learn not to care after a while. they'll never say it out

loud but in the end an indian doesn't count for the same
thing as white people. that they don't even count for as
much as black people.
i did her a favour.
i did them all a favour.
maybe that's not why i do it but still.
it's not the same as with white kids. i mean i'm not a racist
or anything i don't think i'm a racist but the sad truth is it's
true and that's why they make the easiest victims. i've got
nothing in particular against indians. they're just easier to
kill and get away with it.
hell even if i got caught i might get off.
that farmer stuck a shotgun to that boushie kid's skull and
pulled the trigger. got off completely. they used to dump
drunk indians in the snow and leave them to die and they
got away with that too. throw them out of prison in the
middle of winter so they freeze to death and nobody does
anything about it.
all those priests and nuns basically ran concentration camps
for kids. kill the indian save the man. just kill the indian
most of the time.
nobody cares about indians.
the indigenous.
they just don't.
there's not even enough of them to riot. make a fuss.
we've been screwing them from the time we came to these
shores and in the end we just kept getting away with it.
you got statues and faces on money for people who killed
indians abused indians and even killed off an entire species
of animal the buffalo to starve the indians.
they're not even good enough to be black.

i didn't make that situation. i'm just taking advantage of it.
doing most of them a favour like i said.
the world has always been lousy to indians. well since white
people showed up on the shores. it's always been lousy and
will always be lousy. they're better off dead. especially the
young ones. they are definitely better off dead while they
still don't know that the world is never going to be doing
anything but crushing them.
i'm definitely doing them a favour.
i mean don't get me wrong i like the killing.
i definitely like killing them.
i like killing them a lot.
but the chances of it turning out well for these kids or even
the women is pretty much nil.
i probably like killing the kids a little too much.
that could lead to mistakes. it could turn out to be a problem.
i could get caught up so much in enjoying myself that i forget
to take care of the details or forget to be more careful.
i probably should stop killing the kids. eventually.
even if i never make a mistake if someone catches on to all
these kids disappearing and decides to make something out
of it it could end up being a big problem for me.
i tell myself again and again that i'm going to stop with the
kids but then i see one out there all exposed and so easy to
take and i'm at it again.
i probably like it way too much.
and i probably should stop.
probably.
at some point i should take some time off from killing.
change the pattern a little bit.
not yet.

not yet though.

soon maybe but not just yet.

i'm not under any illusion.

i'm a killer.

i'm good at killing. i was born to kill.

the rest is all just the mask the human being that i pretend to be. i do a pretty good job at that too but it's not any part of who i actually am. it's just a mask a costume that i put on so that i can keep on killing.

for a while in the beginning that bothered me. not guilt exactly but a feeling that i was doing something wrong because everything i knew everything i ever read or had been told said i should feel like i was doing something wrong.

but then i realized that life takes life. practically from the beginning living things have killed in order to stay alive. everything kills. and everyone kills. they might pretend with their prepackaged food or their vegetarian vegan diets but the truth the actual truth is that something always dies in order for us to eat and many things die and are killed for no good reason but laziness and ignorance.

at least i know that i'm killing and i know why i'm killing.

it could be that people like me are a natural product of evolution. maybe way back when and even not that long ago having a predator in your group having someone who actually enjoys killing was a necessary way of making sure the group survives. maybe it was even a way of eliminating the weak in your group. it's not any more crazy than a lot of other theories out there that people take seriously. having a predator inside your group might be a way of preparing for all the predators you're going to encounter outside your group.

or maybe i just like killing for no good reason at all.

maybe i was just born to kill.
i don't know.
it doesn't really matter i guess.
but i really should cut back on killing kids for a while.
not right away maybe.
usually i can go a while after killing one before killing the
next one.
usually i don't need to kill for a while particularly after
killing a kid.
but if another one comes along.
if another opportunity to kill one comes along.
hey i'm only human.
well.
something like human.
something that can pass for human.
at least for now.

Suckers

There's a sucker born every minute.

Every single fucking minute.

The wife doesn't like it when I swear. She keeps a swear jar at home.

I put money in it every day even though we're never going to have kids to give the money to.

She's a good woman.

She's entitled to her delusions after all I put her through. I never mention that the jar doesn't really have a point. Every day I put money in and it just stays there. It just sits there. There's a bunch of them now and they don't do anything but sit there full of money. I don't touch them. She doesn't touch them. We go to church every Sunday and she holds my hand, and I'm just glad that she stayed with me all these years.

She knows who I am. She knows the kinds of things that I do. She knows all about me. I never lie to her. I don't talk about the things that I do and she never asks, but I never lie to her. She knows. And still she stays. Still she loves me.

So let her have her swear jar that gets so full of money that neither one of us will ever touch, that gets so full of money that I keep having to buy bigger and bigger swear jars, and we laugh about that.

She's a good woman.

I guess she's a sucker for loving me, but she's my sucker.

All those other suckers though. All those other suckers with their stupid vacant grins and their pathetic excuses for why their lives have gone to shit or why their lives have always been shit.

Two more for the swear jar.

You're either the sucker or the guy taking the sucker. And I decided a long time ago that I was going to be the guy taking the sucker.

I'm definitely going to find a way to take this particular sucker. Even if he is in jail again. His kid is still there. Just the kid and that dirty goat. I can find a way to leverage that situation. Give a man a lever and he can move the world. Not quite sure how just yet, but I'll figure something out when I get there. I always do.

This way to the Egress, folks.

All those suckers lying to themselves all the time, telling themselves some story about god or the way the world is supposed to work, but in the end the world works the way it works whether they like it or not. Predator or prey. The one that eats or the one that gets eaten. That's the world. That's the real world.

You don't need to grow up on this piece of shit Rez to know that.

Another one for the jar.

I tried arguing once with her once that shit shouldn't be considered a swear word. It's just describing a normal bodily function that we all have to do pretty much every single day. We don't think of sweat or scratch as swear words. They're just things that we do but don't like to talk about. Lots of things like that. More that we don't want to talk about than we do. But I guess that a swear word is whatever we say it is, because we're the ones that get to decide what offends us or doesn't. No matter if it's all phoney and the words people get offended by are the things that they do every day or think about every day but just don't want to talk about.

Let her have that. Sometimes you've got to play by the rules of the game, even if they don't make any sense. And sometimes you just make up the rules as you go. Sometimes you find a way to use the rules or bend the rules a little, and you're a fool if you don't, because someone else will, and you'll end up being the sucker. Someone else will get to feed on the broken corpses of your stupid rules.

My job, in theory, is to make sure that those rules don't get broken or bent too far. But my job in the real world is to figure out how far those rules can be bent and to make use of this badge that they were fool enough to pin on me so that me and mine get the most out of this life, and that we're not the suckers, we're not the prey.

Not like this drunk and his messed up kid.

All that council money now. All the casino money. And these suckers got themselves some free land, a nice house, a boat, and then they go to blowing all the money they got and the money they get every year. It doesn't take a genius to talk them out of that land and that house.

They can keep their boats. But that land is worth something to people who know how to take advantage, and it doesn't matter that those are the people who aren't even allowed to own this land. There's always someone who is. There's always someone who is willing to take the money just to have their name on a piece of paper, and that someone is me. If it wasn't me, it would be someone else.

It was good enough for Joseph Brant, it's sure good enough for me.

This idiot doesn't even have the boat and he burned most of his house down, almost killed that creepy kid. Himself. And even that dirty goat. He doesn't deserve that land. He never earned it.

All these idiots would just sit there in their new houses, the same people that they were when there was no council money and casino money, and do nothing with all that land, with all this valuable border land. They don't know what they've got. They don't know what they've been given. They just know how to lose it.

Suckers.

They see a badge and a uniform, that most of them didn't even bother to vote to give me and they believe anything that I tell them, or they're too scared of the uniform to say no. Either way.

Suckers.

Somebody's going to take their money. Somebody's going to take their land. Might as well be me as anybody else. Suckers are born to be suckered. Prey is born to be eaten. It's not the wolf's fault that the pigs didn't know how to build a house.

I watched my old man drink and piss away everything he ever got. Blamed it all on the white man. Blamed it all on the system. Blamed it all on my mother. Never once looked in the mirror and saw that he was the sucker and it wasn't anyone's fault that he didn't have the backbone or the brains to make something out of himself. It wasn't the Residential Schools or the Church or the Government's fault that he stood there and took it and did nothing but feel sorry for himself.

Wasn't anybody's fault that he was a waste of space. That was on him. He was the sucker. And my mother was the sucker for staying and taking all his shit.

Not me.

Not me.

No, I joined the army just to get off this shitty reserve, off this shitty island. Came back and made something out of myself. Got myself a degree and when they wanted to put me on the council, I took it. When they wanted to put the badge on me I took that too. I'll take more than that the first chance I get. I keep the peace. I can't stop every single asshole from being an asshole, but I do what I can.

Another two for the jar.

Three.

Four.

Keep the laws that matter and bend other ones any way that I can bend them. Law of the jungle.

Stupid people shouldn't be alive anyway. They're out there having babies by the bushel with no money that they earned, and no brains and their kids end up as stupid as them, like cows that don't even know that they're being fattened up for slaughter.

Fuck them.

One more for the jar.

Fuck them twice.

Two for the jar.

They talk about fairness and how the world was a paradise before the white man showed up, but half of us were killing the other half, and half of us are still killing the other half. Booze and drugs and shooting each other when they're drunk or wasted. Running each other down on the road or the river. I've seen it. I've seen the wrecks. I've seen the bodies. The suicides. Some people are just too stupid to be alive, or too weak to be alive, and back in the old days if that was you, you were the one that ended up dead. Now you get to to do stupid things to hurt other people. Kill other people.

We had wars. Our ancestors killed other people's ancestors. Ate some of them. Parts of them. That's what our own stories say. When the priests came here we did the same thing to them. They chose the wrong side so we killed them and we tortured them and cut their skin off and ate their hearts. Cut off Brebeuf's lips and stuck a burning stick down his throat.

Paradise my ass.

Wasn't one then and it sure as hell isn't one now. Maybe a paradise for the winners. Maybe a paradise for the hunters and the killers. Paradise is what you make. Paradise is what you can take. Paradise is for the ones strong enough and smart enough not to be the prey.

Cain killed Abel because Abel was too stupid and too weak to be alive.

Survival of the fittest. Sucker born every minute.

Fuck them.

One for the jar.

If we had a kid he'd be one rich motherfucker.

Fuck.

Two.

Better off than this poor kid. His father would sign anything you put in front of him once you get him drunk. Sooner or later he's just going to kill himself and that kid. Too stupid to be alive. Dumb motherfucker.

Fuck.

Two more.

Just another mean drunk. Just another sucker. And that kid. That kid gives me the creeps. Hardly ever talks. Stands there staring off into space like he's in some kind of trance. Talking to that kid's like talking to that stupid goat of his.

Just stares at you and stares like he sees you but like he sees past you too. You just can't tell what the hell is going on inside that kid's head. Gives me the creeps.

Hell is not a swear word.

Not anymore.

I've seen hell. I know what it looks like.

Definitely not a swear word.

Kid gives me the creeps. Damn goat gives me the creeps too. Damn's not a swear work either. They say it on TV all the time. They say all kinds of shit on TV nowadays.

Fuck.

Two more.

Best thing that ever happened to that kid if I took him in, put him in the system. Living in that burned out house all alone. Not my fault his father's an asshole. That prick sober and locked up is meaner than any rattlesnake and more disagreeable too. But maybe the boy could give me some leverage. Maybe that kid could be useful for something at least.

Prick.

That's a swear word.

Yeah.

It's a swear word.

Fuck.

That jar's going to be full. Our kid would be a billionaire, if we could have one.

Going to have to buy another jar. Put it beside all the other ones.

Kid really gives me the creeps. Probably retarded or something. Be better off in the system.

Car in the driveway. There's a fucking car in their driveway.

Probably that girl. Pretty one. Seen her here before. Heard she's trying to take care of the kid. Not sure why. What her angle is. Don't think she's a social worker or a teacher. Kind of looks like she could be part Indian or maybe Oriental. Hard to tell sometimes. Could be related to the kid somehow. Except she doesn't look like she's from this place. Not sure what her angle is and I don't like people who are up to things I can't figure out.
Going to have to dig into that. Find out who the hell she is and if she's going to be a problem.
What the hell is she doing?
She's just standing in the driveway. Staring at something. Behind the house. Maybe the field. She's just standing there. Bag of groceries spilled out all over the driveway. Can't see what she's looking at. Must be something that matters. She should have heard my car. She hasn't looked back even once, and she's not taking notice of all that mess in the driveway.
What the hell is she doing?
I don't like complications. I fucking hate complications.
One more for the jar.
Two more. Losing count.
I can't see the boy. I can't see anything behind that burned up house. Maybe something happened to the kid. Out here all alone, something bad was bound to happen. Not sure how that breaks down for me. Might be hard to reason with that prick after something like that. Or if maybe something like this'd leave him open to be manipulated.
I don't like complications.
Just stop the car. Sit here for a moment. Try to figure out the situation before I go jumping in.

Fuck. She's looking back at me now. She sees me.

The look on her face. What is that look on her face? Fear? Relief?

Guess I'm going to have to find out.

If I wasn't married I'd fuck the hell out of her.

Shit.

Going to need a whole new swear jar.

Okay.

Hate complications. I really fucking hate complications.

Don't like not knowing what I'm walking into. Only one way to find out, I guess. One way to find out who the sucker's going to be.

This way to the Egress, folks. This way to the fucking Egress.

Going to need a whole new jar.

Going to need some way bigger fucking jars.

Goat

i is like grass stuff that grow then stuff that find eat is thing
that is there thing that try get away thing stuff i try take
away from i is make mad make i is mad mad i is tell i is
throw head at jump at so taking stop if they is go go i is
not so mad not so mad not so mad not has throw head
jump jump stupid two leg stupid two leg is make mad i is
stupidest i is go eat all more eat more stupid two leg but
all time all time all time but when no time all time stupid
stupid ugly two leg in way all time i is like boy but boy i
is like but boy stupid sometime too but like stupid two leg
boy but not so bad but sometime bring stuff eat lot time
bring stuff i is eat still ugly boy okay but not not not give eat
smell two leg stupid two leg boy okay but i is like boy but i
is like grass i is like jump i is good jump i is like eat can can
tasty can i is like tasty can i is like boy not bug too much not
make i is mad too much too much hunger always hunger
stuff that grow not not not find thing but hunger boy bring
thing sometime boy not stupid leg two leg throw i head not
bad but sometime go sometime come always bring thing
eat i sometime stay i follow is boy sometime i not is like
rope neck but i try is eat rope too rope is not let i go is not
let i jump is not let i find eat i is not like rope boy come boy
go not noise too not move too so wait wait wait wait wait
wait boy not come wait wait wait more not come wait wait
not jump i is like jump i is good jump boy eat eat hunger
hunger so hunger hunger boy not come wait wait wait
wait wait then come then eat nice eat feed hunger hunger
boy come food i is eat lot tasty eat no more wait wait i is

throw head no cause anger cause happy boy but come back
scratch behind ear i is laugh i is run i is jump i is like scratch
back ear no rope boy hear lot eat happy happy laugh laugh
throw head boy scratch other ear better better scratch under
chin chinny chin better happy happy laugh laugh laugh
jump climb i is like jump climb i is good jump climb i is
eat jump climb eat eat i is run i is throw head i is eat eat
jump climb eat run eat i is throw head eat eat eat i is like eat
scratch ear many thing i is like so many thing make mad but
like stupid two leg stupid stupid two leg think know thing
make sound make noise so lot noise stupid only two leg
think know think know nothing know stupid stupid stupid
make i is mad so mad not like two leg i is like boy but i is
like boy but two leg ugly so ugly no hair is no mouth is just
teeth is so ugly so ugly only two leg no hair just teeth make
funny sound all funny sound all time noise all noise just
teeth ugly ugly ugly like all like stupid two leg like but not
like stupid stupid ugly ugly like not like but i is like boy but
i is like grass i is like climb i is like jump i is good climb jump
i is i is like eat like chew like run like throw head sometime i
is like but i is like boy but i no is like rope too hard eat but i
no is like alone but time nothing eat nothing climb nothing
jump but all is past rope but world is past rope but so i no
is like i is like when boy is on eat i play with i is nice nice
jump jump throw head i is like grass i is like tasty eat but
but but now two leg come field but come i is ready ready
throw head but i is guard field i is guard boy i is ready two
leg stop but now stop away is ready but boy two leg call at
now not danger call at i is ready guard still but boy go two
leg with but not danger act i is not like i is go go go guard
boy i is guard field i is is go too but but now is two leg lady

is from noise smell beast big ugly smell beast she come always i is not like noise smell beast two leg lady bring eat sometime but i is like eat but sometime two leg lady hide i is not like two leg lady hide eat has eat smell food big noise smell beast i is want go i is want go now boy two leg walk walk but so i too go eat behind but away but i is like eat i is call at boy go go away guard boy i two leg but i is go go away eat nother noise smell beast now bad two leg two leg not like not good i is call boy two leg go go two leg lady call now scare call scare scare eat fall good eat fall i is call bad eat fall bad scare call bad two leg call danger call i is call bad danger scare scare boy two leg stop lady two leg call scare scare bad two leg danger mad now call boy two leg stop i is stop all stop stop stop two leg lie down ground boy run boy run scare i is go boy food fall away boy go i is go i is not like i is not like i is go go but boy go boy run now all two leg away i is go is guard boy boy go i is go i is run boy is run i is not like i is not like run run leave eat most like run but but but i is go boy is go i boy is go go go run run go go go away run go go i is go away is go go go away go go go go i is go boy is go boy i is go go go go away is go away is run run go go away i is go with boy but i is boy is two leg is run run run run go go run run run

The Broken Man

We never did make it to the creek.

I never really thought we were going to make it there anyway.

I never thought that the broken man would make it all the way without falling down.

In the end him falling down had nothing to do with it.

We were almost halfway across the field. He was stumbling along and looking like every step was going to be his last one upright, but he kept on walking.

We were near the plastic wading pool with the cartoon whales on it.

I remember that.

I never knew where that pool came from. It was there for as long as I can remember. Since the beginning of time. Like that stupid pool filled up with dirt and old dog shit and skeletons of dead animals and the flies always buzzing around it just belonged exactly right where it was. During the winter there'd be ice and dead field mice stuck in the ice. It was all cracked and covered in dirt but you could still see the cartoon whales even though they were faded and you could tell the pool used to be blue, but it wasn't the blue that you could see now or the blue that it was supposed to be.

The broken man stopped and was looking down at the pool like he wished it was full of water instead of dirt and shit and dead animals.

He was still kind of swaying back and forth and staring down at the pool.

You could hear the river making lapping sounds at the rocks from there. You couldn't hear the creek but you could hear the river.

I could almost feel how thirsty the broken man was. I could almost taste his thirst every time he tried to lick his lips, so dry, and his tongue fat and bloated with thirst. I didn't think he was going to be able to take another step. I was sure he was going to fall down right then just from the thought of the water and I still wasn't sure if I was going to do anything about it.

He was skinny, but still too big for me to carry or drag.

I could go to the creek myself and bring him some water, but I wasn't so sure if I would.

That'd be a lot of work.

I didn't know him. I didn't owe him anything. And I didn't know if he wouldn't do something bad once he had some water in his belly. I wasn't sure if I cared what he did, but it seemed like a lot of trouble to bring him water just so he could do me bad. It seemed like a lot of work for something and somebody I didn't care about one way or another.

He stood there for a while swaying back and forth, looking at that dirty plastic pool and probably listening the river, maybe thinking about the water he couldn't make it to or drink even if he could make it there.

Nobody in their right mind would ever drink from that river no matter how clean it looked. Factories still dumping chemicals in there. Just not the chemicals that makes the river stink and change colour.

And then the broken man took one little step.

And then another step.

I was surprised at that.

Even Goat looked surprised that he took another step.

I was sure he was done. I was sure he was going down. I was sure he was going to fall down right there and never be able to get back up.

But he didn't.

He took a couple of steps and then he took a couple of more, and I followed him and then got out ahead of him again.

That was when the racket back at the house started.

At first it was just people showing up. A car pulling up and then things falling down. I heard it but I just figured it was Dianne and I was keeping my eyes on the man to see if he was going to fall down. She was probably just leaving food again, in the place that I showed her. Maybe some clothes. And maybe she dropped some things. It was better if I didn't have to talk to her anyway. She did her best but there was always those questions in her eyes, and the worry too. It was always better if I didn't have to talk to her. That's why I showed her the hiding place. Sometimes I would see her coming and I would go off just so I wouldn't have to see all the questions and worry in her eyes.

Reminding me who I was. Reminding me what I was.

Goat started to call out. She knew Dianne always brought food. I'm guessing Goat would have preferred if we went back to the food.

Then I heard another car pull up. I wanted to look then, but I was sure the broken man was about to fall down and I didn't want to miss that.

There was a little pause and then the screaming started.

The broken man turned around.

He turned in this slow strange way, where he moved his body instead of turning his head, and I thought he was going to fall, but then I wanted to look too.

I saw the cop.

The one that was in charge of the other cops.

We didn't call him Chief because the Island already had a Chief, so most people called him Captain. He didn't seem like a Captain to me, so I didn't call him anything at all. Not to his face. He was just a cop and him showing up was never good for anybody. He always acted like that badge and uniform made him the big cheese but he was just one more bad guy on the Rez looking to take whatever people have left. He looked more like an Indian than most, even though he was only about a quarter Indian, if even that. But it was on his mother's side so he got to say he was an Indian and looking like an Indian sure helped him get that badge. He was always smiling like he was your best friend but I'd seen enough of him to know he wasn't anybody's friend but his own. He was usually after my father or my uncles but sometimes he just showed up because he got it in his head again about sticking me in some home.

There usually wasn't enough in it for him to bother for long though.

So far.

And he was a little scared of Goat.

Goat head butted him right in the nuts one time. He walked right past Goat without greeting her.

Everybody knew you had to say hello to Goat if you didn't want her to go after you. It was just good manners, even for a goat. But he went charging by and she caught coming back out.

He went down like a sack of bricks.

That was a funny day.

That made me smile.

Goat had a way of making me smile more than most things or most people did.

The cop was standing there holding Dianne by the shoulders and she was screaming and pointing at us.

I couldn't figure out what she was so upset about.

I know she tried real hard but she did get upset pretty easy an awful lot. That's how anyone could tell she wasn't from the Rez.

I stood there and the broken man stood there and the two of them kept looking over at us like someone had died or somebody had robbed a bank.

A bank in the city. Not on the Rez.

The cop let go of Dianne's shoulders with one hand and kind of reached for his gun.

I felt more than saw the broken man's body sag like he knew exactly what was coming.

I just stood there.

I didn't know what was going on. I couldn't figure out why everyone was acting the way they were acting. Sometimes people are nothing like anything I can understand. Most times people are a mystery to me.

Most times I'm a mystery to me.

That's why I like having Goat around. Goat makes more sense than most people.

The cop pulled out his gun.

The broken man fell to his knees and put his hands behind his head without being told.

Dianne kept on screaming.

Goat was screaming now too.

The cop looked confused at first, like he couldn't figure how whether to stay with Dianne and try to calm her down with

the gun still in his hand, or come after us. But I still couldn't
figure out why he would want to do that, or why he had his
gun out.

I'm not stupid.

I knew that they thought that the broken man was danger-
ous.

It was just so obvious to me that he wasn't, and it seemed
stupid to me that they thought he was. I could never figure
out how people talked themselves into so many stupid
things.

The cop lifted his gun up a little like he was going to point
it, and then stopped, still looking like he couldn't figure out
what was going on. He told the broken man to lie down on
his stomach and keep his hands behind his head, and the
broken man did that. The cop didn't yell. But his voice was
shaking a little.

He told me to walk towards him but I just stood there.

He seemed more dangerous with that gun to me than the
broken man ever was.

He said it again and the broken man told me to do it. His
face was in the dirt and his voice sounded funny coming
through the dirt.

I still didn't move.

Goat was screaming and Dianne was screaming and the
cop was pointing his gun.

There was too much stuff coming at me all at once.

I was all filled up with the stupidity and the nonsense of
what was happening.

When I get filled up like that all I want is to get away from
people so that's what I did.

I turned and ran back into the woods. I needed to leave all that screaming and all that craziness behind me. Trees don't yell at you and birds don't tell you what to do. Even bears make more sense than people. The woods were always the safest place that I knew.

I could hear all the screaming and the shouting and then a gun shot and all I knew was that it didn't make any sense and it was all too much of nothing, so I just kept right on running.

My Grandmother told me that in the old days the People would outrun the British and the French. They would run for miles without getting tired. White men called them Indian Runners. The People called them the Dog Runners because they would walk and run and walk and run without stopping the way a dog or a wolf or a coyote would do.

I wondered how far I could run without rest or sleep or food before I would fall down dead.

I wondered how far I could run before I would never have to turn around and come back.

I wondered how far I could run before all the noise in my head would just stop.

I wondered if Goat was following me.

I wondered if the broken man was still thirsty.

And I just kept on running.

The Man

i saw the cop and the woman screaming and i saw him draw
his gun and i fell to my knees and laced my hands behind my
head. all i could think about was that i was thirstier than i had
ever been in my entire life and i didn't want to die thirsty.
i never cared much about living. i just didn't want to die
thirsty.
not that thirsty.
the cop yelled at me to lie down on the ground and i did
that. the woman kept on screaming.
as far as i knew i didn't do nothing wrong but that never
stopped anyone before and i didn't think for a minute that
it was going to stop him from killing me. i locked my fingers
behind my head and waited for the bullet.
i thought about what it would feel like.
been stabbed. been punched and kicked and none of it ever
felt like your thought they should. sometimes no pain at all.
sometimes just some kind of dull thud and ache inside or this
feeling like you're feeling pain from somebody else's body.
like it doesn't belong to you.
sometimes a lot worse than you expect but mostly the pain
comes after. sometimes a little bit after and sometimes a little
more after and sometimes not for hours and sometimes not
for days.
been shot at but i never actually been shot.
that probably hurts different.
i kept waiting for the cop to shoot but he didn't shoot right
away.
i heard him tell the boy to come to him.

i told the boy to go to the cop.
i was pretty sure the cop would shoot me anyways especially
if that woman kept screaming. i would of shot her but the
cop would probably shoot me. but if the kid moved at least
he could get clear. most people don't exactly shoot straight
when there's a lot of commotion.
the cop might know how to shoot.
he probably didn't.
at least the kid could get out of the way.
cop shot my uncle charlie when he was stabbing his wife.
uncle charlie was stabbing the wife. i hated that bitch.
charlie's wife. cop emptied his whole clip into charlie.
everybody wanted to sue except me. i saw charlie when he
was off his rocker and all the way over to crazy.
i never blamed the cop. i would empty my gun too.
i didn't feel nothing bad about this cop either. he just
knew what he saw and with all the shit going down all the
screaming and the kid i probably would shoot me too.
i told the boy to go to the cop but he just stood there.
he stood there for a long time.
i had my face deep in the dirt. I could taste some kind of
animal shit and there was bugs biting at my legs but i kept
still and i told the boy to go to the cop again.
don't know if the kid heard me or understood what i was
saying.
somebody was going to get shot.
better me than the kid.
i just wanted him out of the way so when the cop started
shooting he didn't get hit with a bullet meant for me.
i don't know how the woman kept on screaming. I don't
know don't how she didn't lose her voice.

then the kid turned and started running the other way.
i could see him out of the corner of my eyes and i could hear
him running.
i didn't say nothing.
i just waited to get shot.
i didn't blame the kid neither. he was just a kid and kid's do
stupid things and most often they don't mean no harm.
i just laid there in that dirt with the bugs biting at me and
waited to get shot.
that's all i did.
there was a long time or at least it seemed like a long time
where nothing else happened. i stayed down there with my
face in the shit and dirt and the woman kept on screaming.
maybe there was some words in there but i couldn't tell what
they were if there were any words. maybe she called out the
kid's name. i can't remember it or i didn't understand it if
she did but it seems like she might of called out the kid's
name somewhere in there.
that went on for a while and i didn't feel nothing towards
nobody except by then i was starting to wish the cop'd just
get it over with so i could stop breathing in all that shit and
dirt so i could stop feeling so bone shaking thirsty.
then he started talking to the woman. the cop. he tried to
calm her down and i started thinking that if his attention
was on calming her down then maybe he wasn't going to
get around to shooting me after all.
eating all that dirt and shit was making me a whole lot more
thirsty.
more thirsty than i could ever tell anyone about.
i don't think i was ever that thirsty in my whole life.
i can't remember ever being more thirsty than that.

i don't think i was ever once as thirsty as i was right then.

but i didn't move. i knew better than to move when a uniform was involved. now way of telling what was gonna set them off. for all i knew the cop might be alright. but put a uniform on a guy and he's gonna have to show you why he's got the uniform.

i got nothing against the police.

they framed me up more than once and i took more than my share of beatings from cops and prison guards. black bag over the head so you can't say for sure who it was. even got the phone book treatment case you thought that was just a joke. banging on me with their clubs through a phone book. maybe now they use something else. with phone books getting rare.

but i always chalked that up to people being people. given a chance to get away with it most of us would do the wrong things.

cops.

jail guards and prison guards.

criminals.

all the same when you come down to it so i never held anything in particular against the police.

i get nervous when i see a cop.

but i don't hate them.

not even rez cops who can be the biggest pricks or the most understanding depending on who you run into. this cop could shoot me flat out and get away with it if he really wanted especially when i got up and started walking and then started running the cop might be a prick in some ways and a pretty good guy in others. he coulda shot me just out of panic.

but he didn't.

i got to the woods and i don't know why but i started following the kid's tracks. not hard to track a kid and a goat running through the woods and i still could remember for some reason how to read sign even though i can't remember the last time i tried or the last time i hunted. i stopped hunting soon as i didn't need to kill to eat but i don't remember when that was but i remember i kept tracking even after i stopped hunting for at least a while but i don't remember how long. people are the easiest animal to track unless they don't want to be and this kid and the goat didn't seem to be thinking about throwing off any trackers and i could hear them every now and then.

i guess maybe i was worried the kid would hurt himself somehow. why i followed him. that he could fall somewhere some way or run into a tree or a boulder or something. truth is most indians are no better in the bush than most people and i didn't know nothing about this kid other than that he was going to get me some water and he ran away when everybody started yelling and he was mighty scrawny making me think maybe he could break bones easier than most.

or maybe i was just thirsty maybe i just didn't know what else to do so i started following the kid and the goat.

i don't know.

i don't know why i do half the shit i do truth be told.

at some point the woman stopped screaming and the cop didn't come right after us. i was pretty sure i'd hear a cop that size following us in his cop boots and cops mostly can't do anything without barking orders and yelling at people particularly when they get to chasing them. my guess is that he was smart enough at least to realize that chasing people blind into the woods with a gun is just not the smartest thing to do. a city cop or state or provincial might be stupid enough to try that kind of thing but a rez cop probably would know better.

i figured this rez cop was a lot of things but probably not stupid.

i broke from a kind of lope to a fast walk. can't do much faster than a lope nowadays. i couldn't hear the kid anymore but i could still see sign. pretty recent. he wasn't running into things or over things and it looked like he slowed down from an all-out run to a jog or a fast walk. i wasn't going to catch up to him unless he stopped but he wasn't too far ahead.

i still didn't know what i was gonna do if i caught up to the kid. i still didn't know why i was following him exactly. maybe to make sure he wasn't hurt or wasn't gonna get hurt. maybe just because i didn't know what else to do or maybe i was hoping the kid'd take me to something to drink.

i could hear crows up ahead. lots of times crows will follow people in the woods in case they leave any food behind because crows know people drop shit and just throw shit away. the old woman would say that crows like to laugh at people count of we walk on two legs but can't fly and we're always dropping stuff or throwing it away. crows don't throw nothing away and that's the real reason they follow us.

they must get a real kick out of me. falling down again and again and getting up my face full of dirt.

i swear once upon a time a long time ago i could move through the bush without making a sound or falling down even once.

maybe that's just a dream or some shit i made up in my head. they say every time you remember something you change it just a little. and my memory is sketchy on my best day. so even what i remember how i remember it is probably not how it happened.

i just kept following the kid and the goat. falling down and getting back up to follow some more. maybe it didn't make sense but nothing makes sense to me anymore.

maybe it never did.

one point i fell into a pretty big hollow face first. didn't break anything but i could feel blood and burning across my face from scraping it when i fell and a pretty good lump over my one eye where i hit a rock or something hard.

i got back up and kept following. i just kept getting up and following.

then the kid stopped.

felt him stop more than hearing or any other way.

i used to feel things that way all the time. i could feel the other fighter ready to attack. getting ready to give up. mostly they give up long time before the fight is finished. in their body and in their heart and maybe i see something or hear something about the breathing or how they move. but felt it before i knew about hearing or seeing.

i lost all that when i started throwing fights. it didn't matter no more so i stopped feeling it out and i just fell down. took the count or tapped out. i used to be able to feel weather and other things like what kind of day it was gonna be for me. things i didn't understand but i knew.

the more i fell down the less it mattered.

i got way lost in selling myself too many ways.

but right then at that moment i felt the kid stop and it was almost like i never sold it all away.

just for that moment.

then i was me again. the sold off sold out worn out washed out me and i broke into a walk because i was so tired. knew he was close and i didn't know why i was even falling him or what i was gonna do when i caught up to the kid.

i wondered if he knew.

wondered if the kid felt things the way i used to because he was too young to have sold off most of his being alive.

i walked and caught up to my breath and wiped the sweat off my face with the back of my hand.

felt the kid and the goat just waiting.

nothing ever waited for me.

not that i knew of anyways.

it sure felt like nothing and nobody ever waited for me.

i slowed down real slow.

i knew they were going to wait. i didn't necessarily want to keep them waiting but i didn't want to rush them neither.

it seemed like they deserved for me not to rush so i slowed down.

maybe for the first time in my life. on purpose for the first time not because i couldn't move any faster or because i didn't want to move any faster but because it felt like i should take the time.

i don't remember ever feeling like that.

not in my entire life.

i just slowed down and kept walking and knew that they would wait.

Truth

Some stories are more true than the truth.
Maybe all stories are more true than the truth.
We list off facts and call it the truth. But those are just facts.
The truth is so much larger than facts.
Stories are dreams put into words.
And dreams are more true than we can ever put into words.
We spend a third of our lives dreaming. How can a third of our lives not be true?
We tell stories to share that truth which goes beyond words. We have forgotten how to hear the truths that go beyond words, the truths that fill our stories and our dreams. We have forgotten that there even are truths that can only live in stories and dreams, truths that live in the spaces between words and well beyond the reach of things we can measure or hold in our hands.
Maybe all stories are truer than the truth.
We tell stories to explore the mysteries of life, to explore the great mystery of life. We tell stories to move just a little bit closer to that thing that some of us call God. Stories, real stories, never get where they're going. We journey when we tell stories, but we never arrive.
That is part of the truth of stories.
That is part of the truth of dreams.
We walk in stories. We walk in dreams.
We never arrive.
We never join the beginning to the end.
We live our lives as if we can arrive, as if there is an ending to the story, as if happily ever after is some kind of ending,

some kind of conclusion, not just a leaving off without absolutes or knowing, at best with a kind of acceptance that we can never arrive.

We can only abide.

That is the truth of dreams and that is the truth of stories.

That we can abide with that thing that some would call God but we can never possess it or know it or own it. That we can arrive close to the truth but never live inside of it.

God is truth.

Gandhi said that.

If God is truth then the reverse must be true, that truth is God or something like God, and if that is true then we can never fully know the truth in the same way that we can never fully know God. And dreams and stories, with their blurred edges may also come closer the truth, come closer to God than trying to nail the truth down with facts and certainty, than sacrificing the truth to our need and desire to know, to be certain.

We talk about the truth as if it is something that we can measure and fit in some kind of box of knowing but it is much larger and wilder than that. Real truth doesn't fit in a box or a cage or some hole that we dig for it.

Stories and dreams are truth living free and wild.

There is the story.

There are the stories.

Stories are dreams put into words.

Stories are more true than the truth.

Stories are more real than what we call real.

That's why we tell stories. That's why we listen to stories and read stories. Because a story is much larger and more fleet of foot than a collection of facts and calculations.

Because truth cannot be contained or civilized or trapped.
Because stories help us brush up against the truth. Because
a good story can help us brush up against God.
Some stories are more true than the truth.
Maybe all stories are more true than the truth.
Maybe.
Maybe that's why we tell so many stories.
Maybe that's why we need to tell stories.
Maybe that's why.
I don't know.
I just don't know.
There must be a reason.
I guess that's as good a reason as any.

Gun

In all the years I've been wearing this uniform I've never once pointed a gun at another human being. That's a cliché I know. The cop who never pulled his gun before. But even when I was in country with my military unit I never once had to fire off a round at another human being or even take aim at another human being. I never even liked hunting. I just went along to be one of the boys, but I never really wanted to kill anything when I could just go buy meat at the grocery store.

Part of it was me avoiding action and, more importantly, danger, whenever I could. But part of it too was just that I never ended up in a situation where any of that was required of me. I walked away with a Distinguished Service medal and the word veteran on my license plate, but I never once pointed a gun with live ammunition at another human being before that moment.

This time I came close to pulling the trigger.

This time I came way too close to pulling the trigger and shooting another human being.

Don't even want to imagine the shitload of paperwork that would have meant.

Shitload.

Definitely one more for the jar.

Just for the briefest moment my finger was sliding down toward the trigger and I was actually going to shoot.

When he ran. That was the moment. When he got up and ran and I realized that he was running I almost dropped the girl so I could shoot him. I guess I just didn't want to have to explain why or how I let a guy just run away like that and even though I know that is the wrong reason to shoot another human being I came so close, for just a moment to doing it.

I didn't do it.

Don't know how I ended up with the girl in my arms. Not sure how she got there. Trying to calm her down I guess. To quiet her down. All that screaming was just making the situation worse and I guess I figured if I could get her to calm down I could get control and calm everyone and everything else down too. I guess that's what I was trying to do and it did work, kind of, but don't know if she came to me or I went to her. Just that she did stop screaming. She was shaking like a little frightened bird but at least she wasn't screaming.

But in doing all that I lost sight of the guy and he started to run off.

That was going to mean a lot of paperwork and a lot of fucking explaining to do.

Another one for the jar.

I almost shot him just because I didn't want to have to write it out or explain to anybody him getting away like that. You'd figure once you become Chief of Police, you get to stop answering to people. But there's the council and the Grand Chief and all the other people who are looking for a reason to justify my salary.

I thought about shooting him. I never even thought about shooting anyone before that moment in my entire life. I really wanted to shoot the guy.

I didn't.

I don't know why exactly I wanted to shoot him so bad, other than looking to avoid the paperwork. It was more than the paperwork and the explaining. I mean, it's not like I never got a runner before and it's not like things never got tense before. It's the Rez. Shit happens. But I never once pointed my gun and I never once wanted to shoot somebody as much as I wanted to shoot this guy.

Maybe it was the kid. Maybe that the kid could get hurt by this guy or that people were going to get worked up about me not properly protecting a kid. Maybe I was just pissed at the guy for running and making my life more complicated. I don't know.

Despite being a cop and being ex-military and growing up on the Rez I don't think that I've ever been a violent guy. I've been in some fights. I can take care of myself better than most. But I never really wanted to hurt anybody before, not even when I was a kid.

So I've got this woman, this girl really, shivering in my arms and the kid disappeared into the woods and the guy seeming to follow the kid and my gun's still in my hand and I can't believe how badly I wanted to use it. I mean in a very unhealthy way. I never met this guy before in my life and I barely knew the kid but there I am wanting to go Dirty Harry on some stranger.

She's shivering like a baby bird. She felt as light as one too. If we had a kid, if we could have a kid, she'd probably be about this age. Hopefully a little tougher and not so easy to freak out.

Near as I could tell she was freaking out about nothing much at all. Maybe the guy was a perv and maybe not. For all either one of us could have told he was completely harmless. He didn't exactly look harmless. He looked like somebody who'd been walking on the hard side pretty much his whole life. But he also looked about as run down and beat down as you could get way more than he looked like any kind of danger. I mean I only got a quick look but from what I could tell.

I held her and I holstered my gun real slow. I never even took the safety off, but what was in my head gave me plenty of reason to be cautious and, like I always tell my deputies, always better slow and easy than sorry. So I eased that thing back into its holster and held her with both hands, let her cry it out. Said some comforting shit that I can't even remember.

Shit.

Two more for the jar.

The boy's going to be just fine and everything will be alright and some shit like that.

Another one for the jar.

She cried all over me and then she started to fight me, trying to work loose to go after the boy. I held her tighter and kept saying comforting shit trying to quiet her down. No! No no no! she screamed into my chest. No! Please! I need to... Let me go please!

I eased up my grip on her and then she changed her mind and started trying to push me towards the woods. You have to go! she yelled at me. You have to go after them now! Don't you understand? Don't you understand? He's in danger and you have to save him! You have to go after them now!

I tried to explain that running into the woods, even if I was in any kind of shape to go running after anybody, with a loaded gun at that, was just going to make things worse if anything and the best I could do was round up a search party. But she kept pushing at me and screaming about how

I had to save the kid and I couldn't make her understand that chasing them wasn't going to get anybody anywhere. If the guy was going to hurt the kid it was going to happen with or without my fat ass chasing after them. Truth be told I was very worried that I might end up shooting the guy or missing him and hitting the kid. And maybe me being on his ass would make the guy do something way worse than he had any ideas about doing.

I didn't say that part of course. Scaring her even more wasn't going to help anything.

Instead I held her kicking and screaming with one hand and, after a whole lot of wrestling, managed to call in with the other. Told Delores at dispatching to call in anyone she could think of to form a search party. Delores kept asking if I meant a posse for some reason but I assured her that I meant search party. We didn't know yet that the guy did anything that would call for a posse if things like that still existed. But Delores, being Delores, kept calling it a posse.

I just hoped the girl wasn't one for the nuances of language. She started to calm down then enough so that I could let her go and start gathering up her groceries, getting some order in all that chaos. I explained to her as I gathered up what I could how we were better off waiting and forming a group to find them instead of inflaming the situation. I could see in her eyes she didn't buy that but I could also see that she was calming down enough to realize that she didn't have much choice.

To tell you the truth I wasn't so sure I was right.

I just knew that I didn't want to go into those woods with my itchy trigger finger. And I didn't want to get caught up in that thick forest. Maybe I also didn't want go running

after a guy all on my own. Maybe I knew that I was too old
and fat and lazy to be pulling off that shit.
Another one for the jar.
It wasn't like a stolen purse or catching somebody in the
middle of a B & E. It was more complicated than that.
She was calming down.
She looked deep into my eyes.
Will you find him? Will you save him?
I smiled as gently as I could. Didn't answer. I had been a
cop, and a politician for long enough to know better than to
make promises I couldn't keep.
I hoped we would find the boy.
And I hoped that we would find him alive.
I wasn't sure we would.
And I wasn't sure enough to say.
I definitely was not fucking sure enough at all.
Shit.
That's two more for the jar.

How Crow Made Human Beings

This is a story about Crow.
This is a story about Tsó:ka'we.
She's never up to no good that Crow.
Always stealing things. Sitting up in a tree laughing at
people and all the other animals that can't fly.
She might sneak right out of this story and make trouble
when you're not looking.
She might sneak right out of this story and steal your socks
or your watch or your favourite pen.
She's sneaky that Crow.
She's what you call a Trickster.
You gotta keep your eyes open and count all your fingers
and toes when that Tsó:ka'we is around and especially
when she's being talked about because that opens a door
or a window for her to sneak in and peck away at you.
It was Crow that made human beings. Mostly because she
was bored and when Tsó:ka'we gets bored that's when
she makes the worst kind of trouble.
And that Crow never made worse trouble
than human beings.
She's still laughing about that one.
That one might be the best trick
that Tsó:ka'we ever pulled.
That trick started one day when Crow was bored like I
said and she was flying around Turtle pecking at him and
making fun of him for carrying
the world around on his back.
What a stupid thing to do Tsó:ka'we said.

Why would you carry anything if you don't have to.
Why would you carry the whole world on your back
if you didn't have to.
Turtle wasn't arguing with Crow and just pretty much
ignoring all the pecking and cawing.
Turtle's like that.
Not too much gets to her.
Not even carrying around the whole world.
Turtle isn't much fun as far as Tsó:ka'we is concerned.
And she sure didn't help with Crow's boredom.
So Crow's crazy trickster brain went to work coming up
with things she could do.
Things that might make Crow happy.
Things that might make Tsó:ka'we laugh.
No good things.
Trickster things.
Crazy Crow things.
Crow started out playing in the mud on Turtle's back.
The mud and the clay on Turtle's back.
Crow doesn't like getting dirty. She spends a lot of time
cleaning and preening. She likes to keep her feathers
glossy black. But she loves getting other things dirty. She
loves making things as dirty as they can get.
So there Tsó:ka'we was playing around in the mud and
the clay looking to get something good and dirty.
That's how it all started.
That's how human beings got started.
In the dirt and the mud.
That Crow was throwing mud and clay and sticks and dirt
around when something started to take shape.
The first human.

When Crow saw that, when she saw what she had made,
at the new kind of trouble that she had made,
she thought I should make another one so that it can
trouble the first one. And then another so that they could
gang up on each other. And then she made them into
different sexes so that they could really misunderstand
each other and then different tribes with different
languages so that they would have good reason to hate
each other and fight each other and she made
the different skin colours too
so that they would think that they had even more reasons
to fight and hate and trouble each other.
By the time Tsó:ka'we was done there were so many
different kinds of humans and so many different kinds
of trouble that they could get into.
This time I really outdone myself Crow cawed. This is the
best most troublesome thing that I ever made.
She flew up into a tree and laughed and laughed.
Those human beings were so much trouble
they even got on Turtle's nerves.
They did all these things that they thought were good and
important but were really just trouble and mischief.
The difference between human beings and Crow and
Coyote and Rabbit is that Tricksters know that they're
Tricksters, they know that they're making trouble.
But human beings make all kinds of trouble, so much
trouble that they even get on Turtle's nerves,
and think that they're doing things
that are important and good and helpful.
Those human beings are way crazier than Coyote
or Rabbit or even Crow.

Those human beings are so funny that Crow never
stopped laughing since she made them.
Human beings been nothing but trouble for Turtle
since the day they got made.
They're so funny and so much trouble that
Tsó:ka'we is still laughing today.
She laughs about human beings every single day.
That Crow she sure likes to laugh.
That Tsó:ka'we she sure knows how to make trouble.

Following

i is follow the boy because i is like follow boy and man follow boy so i is follow man and is follow boy boy is run and run then is stop running man is no run he is walk i is pass man and then i is stop i is stop i is stop so i is can follow man so i is protect boy so i is stop i is stop and i is lets man walk past even though even though man is walk very slow i is can feel he no want hurt boy but i is protect boy anyway i is protect boy anyway i is hit man if he is hurt boy and i is protect boy i is not trust man any man any two leg except boy i is trust boy and i is like boy but no other two leg because two leg not even know that they is stupid stupid stupid two leg is think they smart and two leg is do bad thing to other two leg and to not two leg all time all time two leg is do bad thing not two leg is do bad thing too but two leg is do so much bad so much bad so i is watch man i is lets man walk past then i is follow he is follow boy and i is follow man i is follow both i is slow down and i is follow both i is follow both i is can run fast i is can run fast fast faster than man but i is stop i is stop and i is let man pass and then and then i is walk but i is want is run boy is catch boy i is follow boy i is want follow boy not man not man but i is need follow man not boy not boy i is want follow boy but i is follow man so i is protect boy i is watch man so i is follow man not boy man not boy boy boy is important is good is mostly good boy is mostly good so i is like boy i is protect boy i is fight for boy i is let man pass man is walk pass man is sick is broke bad broke bad broke smell bad broke smell bad broke man is not run man is walk funny even for two leg sick is walk

broke is walk man is broke walk but is follow boy i is follow
broke man and i is watch watch watch is protect boy i is
protect boy is watch man is watch broke man sick man man
stop walk is stop walk is almost fall down but then is walk
broke walk sick walk boy up head is stop come is stop and
man is catch up i is catch up is follow sick man broke man
i is watch i is follow is walk walk while man is walk and is
stop when is get to boy so is stop and boy and man make is
noise with face is noise is make each other mouth and is face
is make noise at each and is make noise to is because man
is make noise boy is make noise with face with mouth so i
is make noise with face with mouth and boy is make noise
with face and i is watch i is wait and i is watch i is guard i is
wait all is make noise with face lots noise with face i is watch
i is guard i is wait man is stand boy is stand so i is wait i is
stand too i is stand and i is wait because boy and man is
stand and is wait i is not like wait i is hate wait i is like to go
go go go go but boy is stand and man is stand so i is stand i is
wait but i is not like wait i is rub head on dirt and i is scratch
bum on tree and is rub head on dirt some more i is not like
wait i is not like stand is just stand but i is stand and i is wait
because boy and man is stand and is wait and boy and man
is make noise each from mouth i is not understand noise is
from mouth from face from boy and man they is make soft
noise to each and they is stand and is make soft noise and i
is rub head on ground and i is wait and i is wait and i is wait
but i is not like wait but i is wait and i is wait and i is wait
wait wait wait not like wait is not like wait but but but i is i
is wait wait wait and wait wait i is wait not like wait is wait
but not like wait but is wait wait wait is wait wait for now i
is not like but i is wait i is wait i is wait

Tending Memory

i see the boy first.
the skinny boy.
the beautiful boy.
i am coming from visiting one of my very favourite places.
the old abandoned residential school and its grounds and
its unmarked graves that my father told me about when
he was a caretaker and when they knew what to do with
indians he said he took what headstones there were and
even the rotting wooden crosses off of the graves and then
he brought me here deep in the woods where no one ever
goes any more where even the roads have been left to rot
over but i like to come here and lie in the long grass near the
broken down buildings and just feel all the suffering that
still lingers or maybe i just imagine it.
i'm walking back and here is this beautiful boy wandering
alone through the woods all alone almost right into my
arms like a gift from god a boy so beautiful he could almost
be a girl big brown eyes and dark skin and i see him here
deep in the woods and i think he must be a gift.
but then i see the old man the scarred up man following him
and i think the man must be after the same as me and i feel
so angry it seems so unfair that he should get this beautiful
boy that i think i will kill him when he's done with the boy i
will kill him somehow and then there's a goat this scraggly
goat with them as well and the goat looks right at me even
though i have already hidden. i hate goats. they smell ter-
rible. they sound terrible. they have evil devil eyes.
i have always hated goats. disgusting filthy animals.

the man is almost as ugly as the goat. he is all scars and roughness like he has been banging his head against the world for his entire life. he worries me. he carries himself like he might have have been a fierce one once. like someone who could still put up a fight.
i'd have to sneak up on him.
i don't see any weapons on him and i have my knife good and sharp but i still would prefer my odds if i snuck up on him just to be good and safe. how to do that and not have the pretty boy run away before i can catch him and have my fun with him is the real question. be a real shame to have the beautiful boy get away somehow.
it is hard to tell if either one of them are indians.
indigenous.
it's getting very hard to tell the indigenous ones from the white ones nowadays. makes it difficult for folks like me. hard to identify my favourite prey.
the boy has that golden brown skin, those big brown eyes and that glossy hair that almost seems to reflect the light, but he could easily be a dark skinned white kid, an italian or portugese.
the man was dark skin but it could be from the sun and his head is bald and scarred, maybe shaved or maybe he has some kind of cancer. he could just be a white guy who spent too much time in the sun.
but the fact that they're both here on the reservation so close to the old school probably means they're both indians.
indigenous people.
that's good for me with the boy but maybe not with the man. some of these grown up indians can be tough and they don't seem to scare as easily as white people. maybe just

because most of them have seen a lot more by the time
they've grown up than most whites.
my father may he rot in hell for all of eternity used to like
saying you can't sneak up on an indian. i don't know if that's
true or not. i can move pretty quietly and sneak up on most
people but that thought has got me second guessing moving
on this guy. that and the fact that he and the beautiful boy
are facing each other. that's going to make it real difficult to
take him out without losing the boy.
the man says something to the boy.
the boy doesn't answer, but the goat bleats.
i'm definitely going to kill the goat too.
whether i have to or not. i'm definitely going to kill that
filthy goat.
the man says something else.
the boy still doesn't answer.
neither does the goat.
i start to plan my way to get behind the man. that's the key
to sneaking up on people. plan your moves before you make
them. plan your route. look for obstacles. look for things
that might make noise underfoot. in this case find a route
that'll allow me to move without being seen by the boy.
i don't like that goat being there.
i don't like that goat being there one bit.
in fact, i might like the goat being there even less that the guy.
i'll probably get a little bit of pleasure out of killing him. i
like killing indians. indigenous people. even if they're not
kids. i won't get any pleasure out of having to touch that
filthy goat. i'll be happy it's dead once i kill it but i'll have
to take a long hot bath to get that goat smell off of me once
it's done.

mind you, the guy doesn't look like he smells all that great
either.
definitely going to need a bath.
going to need a bath anyway after i'm done with the boy
but it's just a shame that experience is going to be spoiled
by the stink of goat and maybe some old beat up homeless
indian.
indigenous guy.
person.
for a while they just stand there. the guy not talking. the
beautiful boy not talking which i really really like about
him. it makes me wonder if he will be that quiet when i
have him. if he'll scream at all. or beg. something about
him tells me that he won't and that excites me greatly. i like
when they're stoic. when they hold it inside. when they
fight the pain and the suffering. it makes those little flickers
of suffering in their eyes so much more precious, so much
more beautiful and sexy which is why i like the indians so
very much.
the indigenous ones.
they just stand there quietly and the goat bleats every once
in a while.
goats are not quiet animals. it's just one of the many things
that i despise about them. they're filthy and they're stupid
and they have strange demon eyes and tongues that always
seem to be sticking out somewhere which is just very rude
and they have a habit of charging at you for no reason at all,
of quite literally butting in where they're not wanted. i hate
everything about them and they stink.
so i will definitely kill the goat even if i have to hunt it down
after i'm done with the other two.

while they're just standing there quietly i'm carefully planning my route step by step to get behind the guy without getting seen and without making any noise. and then i think about the best way to kill the guy. it's important to plan that too. particularly when there are multiples involved because you want to get him done quickly enough that you can catch the boy if he does try to flee all the while making sure that the guy is well and truly out of action if not altogether dead. it can be fun to drag it out. but in this case would it be worth dragging it out with the guy if it means risking losing the beautiful boy?

no.

no no no no.

no the guy will have to die quickly.

can't risk him messing up my time with this beautiful quiet boy.

most people think that slashing the throat is the fastest and best way to kill someone because they've seen it so often in the movies but if you don't cut deep enough it can take minutes and the person can still put up a fight, not mention how messy and slippery it can get with blood spraying everywhere. it's a way to kill someone but definitely not the best way if you want to make it quick and sure. the best way from behind is to lift the chin and stab upwards and backwards right under the chin driving right into the brain. a lot less blood and it's over in a matter of seconds liking flicking a switch and just clicking the person off. you have to have a good sharp knife with a good long straight blade which is exactly what i have.

the body will sag and i'll walk over it to grab the boy and the fun will begin.

i've got the route and the obstacles and how to kill the guy.
now it's just a matter of doing it.
easy peasy.
and so close to the old school. life doesn't get much better.
circle around through the trees not rushing it never rushing
it watching for obstacles or anything that might make noise
underfoot. step soft and easy toe to foot feeling each step
before i put my weight down circling wide and slow around
them while they just stand there. someone coming in the
distance but they're coming very slow and very heavy. i'll
have to move the beautiful boy, but other than that, it's not
a problem.
i wonder why they're not speaking to each other.
i stop to look at them. the guy is staring at the ground and
the boy is looking at the guy but not speaking. even the goat
is not making any sound. i don't know what they're doing.
maybe i was right. maybe the guy is after what i'm after.
no.
i don't think so.
he's a rough looking customer, but i think he's looking at
the ground to let the boy know he doesn't mean any harm
and that he's not going to do anything the boy doesn't want
to do. i don't think they know each other but they seem to
be talking to each other without words somehow without
even both of them looking at each other. almost like they're
two versions of the same person or something crazy like
that. at least that's what it seems like to me. like from a
movie. or a dream.
it's so strange that i get frozen by it for a little bit.
then the sound of the other person or people coming up on
us gets me going again.

i get back to circling, careful not to make a sound or to be seen. this is what i do. i'm good at it. i was born to be good at it.

i was born to hunt other human beings.

i creep behind trees. behind rocks. behind bushes and brambles. before each step studying the earth before me for pebbles or leaves or fallen debris. anything that might make a noise underfoot. i pause now and again to see if they have moved or taken notice of me but they are almost as still as statues.

and then, when i am close, oh so close, when i have my nice sharp knife already in my hand, the filthy ugly goat looks right at me with those demon eyes and i know what it's going to do even before it does it because it is a goat and goats are awful terrible filthy things.

it bellows at me.

the ugly awful thing bellows at me.

and the man turns and he sees me and the boy turns and he too sees me and i charge the last few feet at the man with my knife coming from underneath where he is unlikely to see or expect it but he is both quicker and more aware than he should be or could be and rather than backing up which most people would do he steps towards me cutting off my my space he meets my knife with the back of his arm not the front the way most people would do exposing their arteries and he hits me under the chin and for a moment there is blankness emptiness and i do not know if i am falling or standing if i am still breathing or still conscious there is only blank nothingness.

only blank nothingness.

and then i hear a voice yelling "run!"

and i can feel him moving my arm and i am back and i
see the beautiful boy running from of the corner of my
eye and that awful goat running with the boy and then
my body is back and i am dropping low and driving the
knife under his arm and into his ribs but no i know better
than that no the knife hits bone before it goes deeper and
gets stuck and he and i are looking at each other and he
drives his fist into my throat and oh the pain and i twist the
knife there is blood spraying from his mouth but he hits me
again anyway driving into me with his elbow this time in
my throat driving the knife even deeper into himself and
there is blankness there is blackness there is so much pain
i feeling a burning in my back before i hear a crack like a
gunshot from behind me the burning and i can't breathe
but no i'm the killer i'm the killer i can't no this can't the
beautiful boy that filthy goat if only if only if only blackness
burning my back throat.
and there is.
there is.
falling.
falling.
so much.
falling.
i don't don't want to die i don't want to die please please
please i don't want to die i'm not supposed to die please
please it it hurts so so so it please please please not me not
me i i i hate hate hate goats.
and then.
there is.
there is.
please no.

it can't.
i can't.
i don't want to.
please.
there is only.
there is.
only.
only.
falling.

Bear

There was this Bear
This Ohkwá:ri
She wasn't the only Bear or the last Bear
or anything like that
But she was a Bear and that made her something
Something that was supposed to be there
Before people started showing up she had it pretty good
Being an Ohkwá:ri she didn't have much to worry about
Then the people showed up and at first
they gave her respect
But then because they feared her they dug that pit
And she fell in
And they turned her into everything
that wasn't Bear anymore
Once that was done they got bored and buried
her and forgot all about her
Forgot their lives weren't the same without Ohkwá:ri in it
Till one day somebody showed up
and started digging that Ohkwá:ri up
That made everybody pretty upset
The ancestors of the people that buried her
started mumbling apologies
And the ancestors of the Bear just felt
the deep sadness in their souls widen
Lots of people felt it would have been better
if she had been left buried
But lots of other people, not just her ancestors,
knew that the Ohkwá:ri belonged in the world

And we needed to be reminded
that she belonged in the world
The people that dug that hole thought
that they were getting rid of something wild,
something dangerous.
And they were.
But when that Bear fell into that hole they were also trying
to get rid of something very precious,
the whole world almost lost something precious
Something that knew what it felt like to stand up
on your hind legs and roar
Something that knew what it felt like to roam completely
free without boundaries and without fear
Maybe the world felt like a safer place when that
Bear fell into that hole
When they buried it in an unmarked grave
But maybe a world without Ohkwá:ri in it is also a world
without wildness, without magic
Maybe a world without Ohkwá:ri is a world without
dreams, a world that does not know how to look back and
honour the past as well as look forward
Maybe, just maybe, in the act of unearthing Ohkwá:ri, we
are really unearthing the fullness of ourselves.
But the ancestors of the Bear know this
The Ancestors of the Ohkwá:ri know this one thing
You can't remove Bears from the world
no matter how you try.
No matter how many holes you make the
Ohkwá:ri will never go away.
Not really
They can fall in the holes that you dug for them.

You can cover them up and try to pretend
that the graves ever existed.
But some things you cannot just forget about.
Some things will never just be part of the past.
Some buried things will not stay buried.
Some things will seem to fall away
But they will never truly be gone
They will never truly be forgotten
There was this Bear
There is this Ohkwá:ri
No matter how they tried to kill it
No matter how they tried to forget it
No matter how they tried to bury it
The Ohkwá:ri was always there
The Ohkwá:ri will always be there.